MW00413608

Fishing Alaska's
Kenai Peninsula

Fishing Alaska's Kenai Peninsula

A Complete Angler's Guide

Dave Atcheson

The Countryman Press
A division of W. W. Norton & Company
Independent Publishers Since 1923

Copyright © 2002 by Dave Atcheson

First Edition

All rights reserved. No part of this book may be reproduced in any form or
by any electronic or mechanical means, including information storage and
retrieval systems, without permission in writing from the publisher, except
by a reviewer, who may quote brief passages.

Library of Congress Cataloging-in-Publication Data
Atcheson, Dave.
Fishing Alaska's Kenai Peninsula : a complete angler's
guide / Dave Atcheson.—1st ed.
p. cm.
ISBN 978-0-88150-550-4
1. Fishing—Alaska—Kenai Peninsula. I. Title.
SH467 .A83 2002
799.1'09798'3—dc21   2002026123

Maps by Paul Woodward, © 2002 The Countryman Press
Cover and interior design by Faith Hague
Cover and interior photographs by Dave Atcheson unless
indicated otherwise
Text composition by Kelly Thompson
Illustrations by Barbara Smullen

The Countryman Press
www.countrymanpress.com

A division of W.W. Norton & Company
500 Fifth Avenue, New York, NY 10110
www.wwnorton.com

In memory of my mother, Nancy Eaton.

For my stepfather, Ken Eaton, who in his quiet way was always there.

For my Alaskan fishing buddies, Tony Lewis, Richard Kelso, Jerry McDonnell, and Jim Quinn.

And especially, for my very first fishing buddy, George Atcheson. Thanks Dad.

Contents

ACKNOWLEDGMENTS 9

INTRODUCTION 11

PART I: BEFORE WETTING A LINE

1 ~ PLANNING A TRIP TO ALASKA 19

*What to Bring • Selecting a Guide • A Word about Wildlife •
Where to Begin*

2 ~ WHY THE FLY 31

PART II: LAKE FISHING

3 ~ STILL-WATER WONDERLAND 41

4 ~ APPROACHING A LAKE 47

5 ~ EQUIPMENT AND TACTICS 51

6 ~ FINDING A LAKE 55

*The Swan Lake/Swanson River Canoe System • The Swan Lake Route • The
Swanson River Route • Resurrection Pass Trail • Russian Lakes Trail • Johnson
Pass Trail*

7 ~ GOING FOR GRAYLING 75

Crescent Lake • Lower Fuller Lake • Grayling Lake • Paradise Lakes

8 ~ LAKES ALONG THE ROAD SYSTEM 85

*Summit Lakes • Jerome Lake • Tern Lake • Upper and Lower Trail Lakes • Vagt
Lake • Grouse Lake • Jean Lake • Hidden Lake • Ohmer Lakes • Engineer Lake •
Kelly and Peterson Lakes • Egumen Lake • Watson Lake • North Kenai Road •
Cabin Lake• Daniels Lake • Stormy Lake • Stocked Lakes*

PART III: RIVERS AND STREAMS

9 ~ ONE MORE TRY 93

10 ~ APPROACHING A RIVER 99

11 ~ THE KENAI RIVER 105

Upper Kenai River • Middle Kenai River • Lower Kenai River •

Kenai River Rainbow Trout and Dolly Varden • Accessing the River • Salmon Throughout the System

12 ~ TRIBUTARIES OF THE KENAI RIVER 137

The Russian River • Quartz Creek and Ptarmigan Creek

13 ~ STREAMS OF THE SOUTHERN KENAI PENINSULA 145

The Kasilof River • The Anchor River, Deep Creek, and the Ninilchik River

14 ~ THE QUIET ALTERNATIVE 153

The Swanson River • Resurrection Creek

PART IV: SALT WATER

15 ~ RESURRECTION BAY (SEWARD) 163

Ressurection Bay • Finding a Place to Stay

16 ~ KACHEMAK BAY AND COOK INLET (HOMER TO NINILCHIK) 173

Kachemak Bay • Finding a Place to Stay

17 ~ COOKING YOUR CATCH 181

Smoked Salmon Canapés • Baked Salmon or Halibut • Grilled Salmon

INDEX 185

Acknowledgments

Many people contributed advice and encouragement, all of which resulted in the production of this book. Tony Lewis, who graciously waded through much of it. Of course, Kermit Hummel and the editors at Countryman Press. Also, J. R. Sutphin, Andy Hall. Curt Muse, a.k.a. Curt Trout, of Alaska Troutfitters. Mike Miller and the folks at Miller's Landing. The Alaska Department of Fish and Game, specifically Bruce King, Jeff Breakfield, Tim McKinley, and Bob Begich. The U.S. Fish and Wildlife Service: Doug Palmer, Ken Gates, and Charley Weeks. And the people at Alaska State Parks and Kenai Fjords National Park, who have, over the years, answered many questions and have always pointed me in the right direction.

Introduction

I'll never forget the encounter. He was an older gentleman, obviously a fly-fisherman, standing idle on a long stretch of gravel, during the peak of trout season on the upper Kenai River. A long way from his guide and the rest of his party, had he broken his rod? I wondered. Why else would someone, on such a magnificent day, surrounded by such beauty, be so downcast and glum?

His disappointment intensified as he began telling me about his trip, how the agent who booked it had assured him that rainbow trout on the Kenai could readily be taken throughout the year on dry flies.

I informed him that by this time of year (late summer), with so many salmon in the river, the trout had begun to hone in almost exclusively on salmon eggs. I suggested he try an egg pattern. Surely his guide had some.

"No," he flatly refused, looking at me as if I did not understand. I guess I didn't because I kept at him.

"You 'dead drift' them," I said, "just as you would a nymph."

"Oh, I don't fish nymphs," he said, "I'm a fly-fisherman."

He must have seen the bewildered look cross my face. "A *dry-fly-fisherman*," he clarified.

"In this case it might be worth trying a new technique," I suggested.

"I have no interest in this," he said, pointing to the others in his party.

I didn't know quite what to say. I know we each have our own thresholds, rules we devise for ourselves and adhere to. I certainly have mine and can appreciate that this gentleman had his. But, on the other hand, why limit yourself? While in recent years I have become a whole-hearted convert to the fly-rod, and love nothing more than watching a trout cautiously pluck a dry fly off the surface, one of my main objectives is still to catch fish; and I'll often opt for the most effective means of doing so. In many cases that means taking up a bait-

Fish on! The beginning of another Alaskan fish tale

caster and backtrolling for king salmon, jigging for halibut off the coast, or enticing a silver salmon out of a deepwater slough with a favorite spinner or spoon. Part of what has drawn me to fishing, and what keeps me interested, is that there are so many ways of doing it. That's why, while many of these pages are dedicated to fly-fishing, an equal number are devoted to a variety of other methods. One of the aims of this book is to share these various techniques with fishermen of every style, to supply both general and specific information on a vast array of equipment as well as insight into fish behavior. It is my intent to appeal to the occasional and the obsessed angler, to provide some entertaining and exciting anecdotes while providing practical advice that will improve success not only on the Kenai Peninsula, not only in Alaska, but anywhere you choose to wet a line.

When I first arrived in Alaska and on the Kenai Peninsula, with its 25,000 square miles of rivers and lakes, with its ocean, and its five species of salmon returning at different intervals throughout the summer, I found it confusing to say the least. Yet, the first time I saw a moose raise its noble head out of a lily-bedecked pond, or found myself lakeside, flanked by a wilderness worthy of Jack London, I was hooked. Captured by the unparalleled beauty, and by the prospect of landing my first salmon or of tangling with a trout in a land where that 20-inch fantasy is bridged every day.

Since that time I have been on a permanent Alaskan vacation, often having to settle for temporary, seasonal jobs, jobs that have allowed me consecutive weeks, even months in a row off, to explore these rivers and lakes. It's not always been easy, opting for fishing time rather than work, giving up gainful employment to pursue my passion. When the money has run thin and I've been "stuck" on the Kenai Peninsula, I've made the best of it. I've cajoled my way aboard river rafts and charter boats and done my best to extract information from old-timers, following their advice to every far-flung fishing hole . . . and, in the process, learned to catch fish I once only dreamed of. It's taken 15 years, but I'm finally ready to share the results of this intensive (and extremely fun-filled) investigation. And as I sit down to prepare this text I'm reminded of all those who helped—fellow anglers always willing to pass along advice, to share a particular fly, and to spread the good karma of fishing by letting others in on the fun. It's in their spirit, and with the do-it-yourselfer in mind, that I write and that I come to the next objective of this book—letting readers know where to fish.

I will highlight hot spots both on and off the beaten path, giving pointers on how to survive, and actually enjoy, those famous "combat" zones of the Kenai Peninsula. Places like the Russian River, where every year crowds gather to intercept returning salmon. I will point out those large, difficult-to-fish bodies of water, where, with a limited amount of time, the services of a guide might be worthwhile. Each fishing spot has been rated on a scale of 1 to 5, with 5 being the highest rating and 1 the lowest. The "Wilderness Experience" rating refers to how alone you're likely to be in any given spot. I will give advice on how to fish these areas while also steering readers toward other inexpensive alternatives. The lakes, for instance, are a wellspring of angling opportunity that dot nearly every road and trail system, that

The author with a Crescent Lake grayling

color nearly every corner of the Alaskan map. Often the simple act of venturing to these places is reward enough: the chance at the adventure of a lifetime, the opportunity to regain something lost within ourselves, something quiet and primitive, and forgotten in our hectic workaday worlds. It's the opportunity to reacquaint ourselves with a not-too-distant past, where eagle, wolf, lynx, and bear remain free, and where lucky anglers, whether sticking to the main byways for a quick weekend or venturing deep into the bush for an extended stay, can still find themselves utterly alone on a beautiful stretch of water that yields upward of 30 to 40 rainbow trout, char, or Dolly Varden in a single afternoon. And perhaps the real beauty of these places is that they are accessible and that someone with a little outdoor savvy can get to them and fish them on his or her own, and often with the same box of spinners and the same selection of flies used at home.

Finally, this book is an attempt not only to tell readers where or how to fish but to convey some sense of what I hold so dear about living in Alaska, what it is that makes this place unique. When I began writing, I did not set out to produce a typical manual. When I read about fishing a particular place I don't merely want to be told *how* to fish it, but *why* I would want to. I want a story that imparts some of the flavor of a particular region, a story that inspires me to find the places it describes and that, along with the "nuts and bolts," allows me to experience its subject. I hope that's what I've done here. With that being said, I realize the overwhelming excitement of finally reaching a new destination and the need to skip the extraneous information and get right to the meat of the matter—where do I go and which lure or fly do I use. The practical knowledge that is desperately needed is here. By all means use this book as the resource it is intended to be. But when the urgency has subsided and you're sitting back at camp, or at home perhaps, in the final doldrums of winter, in the calm before the fury of the upcoming fishing season, I hope you will come back to the stories interlaced throughout this work. In them I hope you will find a few subtle surprises, tidbits of information that will increase not only your fishing knowledge but your appreciation for this place I cherish, this place I call home.

PART I

BEFORE WETTING A LINE

A quiet fall day on the Russian River

CHAPTER 1

Planning a Trip to Alaska

When scheduling a visit to the 49th state, and the Kenai Peninsula, it is important to begin early and to research your trip thoroughly. And while it is wise to make arrangements well in advance, perhaps the best piece of fishing advice I can give is to have a backup plan, or better yet several backup plans. The most common mistake visitors make is setting their sights on only one type of fishing or one species of fish. Every year, for instance, letters to the editor appear from out-of-state anglers who have come north, for only a week or two, to fish exclusively for king salmon. They bemoan the poor fishing and claim the stories they've seen on television or in print are no more than an elaborate fabrication designed to ruin their vacation and take their money. The fact of the matter is that salmon runs, while well documented, are extremely unpredictable. It's unfortunate, but many an angler's plans have been foiled by a weak or late return.

River conditions can also change drastically in a relatively short period. A little rain, or a hot sunny day melting snow off the mountains, can turn a river murky and wild, throwing the fishing off. This is when it might be time to institute Plan B: perhaps a hike, bike, or fly-in to a lake for some trout fishing, or a chance to try another river where the conditions are better. Timing is everything, and sometimes the only recourse in dealing with Mother Nature is to alter your plans. By being prepared mentally, as well as physically with equipment, for various types of fishing, you have much less chance of going home disappointed.

Another reason many anglers end up altering their plans is congestion. The Kenai Peninsula, because of its proximity to Anchorage, sees its share of people, and many visitors are not prepared for just how crowded it can become along the road system. The fact is that anywhere in Alaska where there is a road and salmon, there are sure to be people. Does this mean there isn't good fishing along the road system? Absolutely not. Fishing along the road system is certainly the easiest and most cost-effective way to fish Alaska. However, if you are unable or unwilling to stray very far afield, you may need to refine that vision of Alaska as the ultimate wilderness experience. There are still, from every vantage point, awe-inspiring vistas, and fishing can be tremendous in the "combat" zones—that's why everyone is there. But when you are fishing these places, be prepared for a social outing; bring a great deal of patience and a good attitude.

Are there ways to beat the crowds, to have solitude, and to still have good fishing? Absolutely. It simply takes an open mind and, once again, the willingness to change both perception and plan. Consider scheduling a trip at some time other than during the peak of tourist season. Be willing to fish a variety of species. Fish at off-hours. Try a trout stream early in the year, before the salmon show up, or late in the year, after they have left. Break out the 3-weight fly-rod or the ultralight spinning outfit and go for grayling. Try fishing Dolly Varden on a stream closed to salmon. Think about fishing silver salmon in September, after the crowds have gone.

Does this mean you have to give up the dream of that coveted king salmon? No way, there's nothing quite like the bend one of these behemoths will put in your rod. Just be prepared for other people and enjoy the company.

What to Bring

Specific fishing equipment is discussed in each chapter as it pertains to each type of fishing, but here are a few general recommendations. Some may seem obvious, but in most cases they are items you won't want to be without. The first is a good pair of Polaroid sunglasses. They are a must for shallow streams and for scouting the submerged weed beds of area lakes. Always have a hook hone. The rocky bottoms of Alaskan rivers can dull a hook quickly. And who wants to lose the "catch of a lifetime" (I should know, I've lost several) because they can't be bothered to take a moment to sharpen the hook? Have a pair of forceps, or for releasing large salmon, bring a pair of needle-nose pliers. Streams can run cold and fast, and a good-quality comfortable pair of waders can make all the difference. Many anglers still wear neoprene, though breathable waders (I absolutely love mine), with the right layering underneath, will stand up to the coldest conditions.

Alaska is notorious for its black flies and mosquitoes, so have an ample supply of insect repellent and perhaps a head net. And, contrary to its reputation as a land of ice and snow, Alaska can become downright hot in the summer so don't forget sunblock.

Some other items worth considering are binoculars and a good camera. Both are made small enough to easily slip into any jacket or fishing vest. Binoculars make taking a break better than going to the zoo, and even if you are not a shutterbug, a camera is a great way to bring a bit of Alaska's magnificent scenery, its wildlife, and its fish home with you. By the way, don't forget a spare battery and a lot of extra film.

One additional item that I find almost indispensable is a small dry bag or day pack in which to stow excess gear. You will want the type of bag you don't mind getting dirty on a streambank or tossing into the bottom of a boat, one with straps that makes it easy to tote along some extra clothes, a spare reel, or any of the aforementioned items.

The Alaskan weather can be erratic. It's not uncommon to be traipsing down a trail on a lovely June morning, wearing shorts and a T-shirt, and only a few hours later find yourself caught in a storm,

RICHARD KELSO

Bundled up for steelhead fishing on Deep Creek

having to don an army's worth of warm clothes and raingear. With these impulsive weather gods, be prepared for anything. Dress in layers that are easily added or shed. In most cases start with polypropylene underwear, followed by polarfleece, and then possibly a vest or coat. Finally, end with a wind shell or raingear. I can't say enough about having top-quality raingear that will hold up to an extended deluge.

Include in your Alaskan wardrobe a decent pair of gloves. Fingerless wool or neoprene gloves are an excellent choice for anglers. There are also a variety of mittens in which the area above the palms folds back and attaches with Velcro, exposing fingers only when you need to tie on a new fly or reel in the big one.

It may sound excessive, but a couple of types of hats are also essential: a large-brimmed baseball-style cap to break the glare on sunny days and a thermal wool or synthetic hat to keep your ears warm when the winds decide to blow. Finally, cold feet are no fun. Finish things off with a good pair of socks. Polypropylene–wool blend socks, although pretty extravagant at $12 a pair, will last several years and, most

PLANNING A TRIP TO ALASKA

important, are the best bet (along with decent footwear) for keeping feet from freezing.

For most fishermen it's easy to become transfixed on the flow of the water, to let fishing take precedence, and to not realize just how cold and wet they are. Wearing proper clothing, paying attention to the surroundings, and adding another layer of clothes can mean the difference between simple discomfort and hypothermia. It's not just a matter of convenience; it's often a matter of safety.

Selecting a Guide

Although this book is primarily for the do-it-yourselfer, there are certain circumstances when you might want to consider the services of a guide. Large rivers like the Upper Kenai, for instance, are constantly in a state of flux, fishing hot spots changing daily with the water level. For those able to fish these rivers only once or twice a season, or a lifetime—or for anyone simply looking to gather some inside information—a guide is well worth the investment. It's a great way to find out what techniques are used locally and to get tips that will be of benefit when you are on your own. Ply the guide with questions; ask where the fish are holding, which fly is hot, and find out how to access certain places yourself.

When selecting a guide it's always important to ask for references, and it's equally important to check them. Call the client list the company gives you and find out what their relationship is to the guide service. How did they come to use this particular company? What kind of fishing did they do? Is it the same type you're interested in? If you are a fly-fisher, does the guide service cater to your needs? Do they understand the type of water you want to fish? What flies will you need and do they supply them?

When deciding on a guide service, it's important not only to inquire about the company's credentials but about those of the individual who will actually be taking you out. The company may have been in business for 20 years, but how many seasons' experience does your guide actually have? How about experience on the particular river you will be fishing? We all have to begin somewhere, but you don't want to be the one who gets stuck breaking in the rookie.

A Word About Wildlife

Sit for a while in a coffee shop, stand in line at the post office, or go just about anywhere people gather in Alaska, and you will be sure to catch a conversation that revolves around wildlife. Sitting at a lodge along the Kenai River one afternoon, I couldn't help overhearing just such a conversation. A couple, obviously just having returned from an outing, was commenting with awe on what they had encountered. They described with great zeal and affection all they had seen, from the scale of the mountains to the variety of birds. "It's just too bad," the woman said. "This place would be great if we didn't have to worry about bears."

I wasn't surprised, having often heard visitors, and even some residents, echo these sentiments. When I do, I'm always tempted to say, "Isn't that what makes Alaska great, that we have the chance to see these magnificent animals?" But, I also understand that this paranoia—or bearanoia—is natural. Any time there's an incident involving a bear, sometimes even a close encounter, it's big news. These bear tales sell newspapers and fill books—there's even a couple in this book. But there is a reason these stories loom so large. It's that they are relatively rare. For instance, I wanted to reassure the woman at the lodge by letting her know how much more likely she is to get into a car accident than even see a bear, that being attacked by a bruin is akin to being struck by lightning.

This doesn't mean that it couldn't happen and that you shouldn't take the proper precautions. Just as you would steer clear of a golf course during a thunderstorm, you should steer clear of an area where aggressive bears have been sighted, or where it's been reported they have a kill—no matter how good the fishing is. Just use common sense when dealing with *any* type of wildlife. Moose, for instance, may appear docile but can be just as dangerous as bears when provoked.

Give any animal its space. Too often confrontations have occurred

A grizzly on the Kenai River

when people try to sneak in for a photo. This is especially true along the highways. Just because an animal is out in the open, along a roadway, does not mean it is any less wild. When you do encounter an animal, be sensitive to its behavior and aware of any abrupt change. Avoid as much as possible the chance of confrontation by making a lot of noise when you hike. Be especially aware of adults with young—a sow with cubs, or a mama moose with calves to protect, is much more likely to be aggressive. Even a nesting spruce grouse, a notoriously timid bird, will defend its chicks with a great deal of gusto.

When you do have an unwanted encounter, it is important to stay calm. Stand your ground at first; don't ever run. When the time comes, back away slowly. Bears are known for their poor eyesight, so make yourself known. Try to look as large as possible. If you're in a group, have the members get together. Wave your arms, shout, or sing. Usually this is all it takes to avoid a confrontation. When the time comes to retreat, back away slowly, move off the trail if possible, and always leave the animal a route out.

Should you carry a gun in bear country? If you are not proficient in the use of a firearm and not fully prepared to use it, don't even consider bringing one; this only increases the chance of injuring yourself or someone else. If you feel comfortable with a gun and feel better having one (I occasionally lug one along myself), choose the right weapon. Many people tote large-caliber pistols because of their convenient size, but they are not the best choice. A hunting rifle, a .338 or .375 caliber, is standard, although a pump-action 12-gauge shotgun loaded with rifled slugs probably offers the best protection. A shotgun can also be fitted with an 18-inch barrel, making it easier to handle in heavy brush.

The Kenai Peninsula is home to a vast array of wildlife: Dall sheep, mountain goat, wolf, wolverine, lynx, black bear, and, of course, grizzly. They should neither be feared nor taken for granted, and we should exalt in the fact that we are able to share this land with them. We should respect what they represent and enjoy their presence, but always in a safe and unthreatening manner.

A moose cow with calves crossing the Kenai River

Where to Begin

Now that you are primed, and know what to bring, it's time to begin researching in earnest. This book is the right place to start. After perusing these pages and deciding where to fish, you may want to return to this section. Here you will find a list of the various government agencies represented on the Kenai Peninsula. With the National Forest Service, National Park Service, Kenai National Wildlife Refuge, and Alaska State Parks, it can be difficult to sort out. Each section of this book, where applicable, will point out which agency has jurisdiction and what services they offer. The Forest Service, for instance, has a wide range of public-use cabins scattered throughout the peninsula. They are a rather rustic but comfortable way to enjoy a few nights of fishing on certain rivers and lakes. Reservations can be made online via the agency's web site. Prices vary, and in most cases reservations must be made early.

Even if you are not looking for a cabin, a great deal of information

A family of Dall sheep on Kenai Lake

on trail conditions, natural history and, of course, fishing, can be gathered either online, by mail, or by visiting these offices in person. I've included various other web sites that supply information on fishing and may be of interest.

The U.S. Forest Service, Chugach National Forest
334 Fourth Avenue
Seward 99664
907-224-3374
Cabin reservations, up to 180 days in advance: 877-444-6777 or www.reserveusa.com

Alaska State Parks, Kenai Area Office
P.O. Box 1247
Soldotna 99669
907-262-5581
South District Office:

P.O. Box 3248
Homer 99603
907-235-7024
Cabin reservations, up to 180 days in advance: Application is available online, but must be made in person or by mail.
www.dnr.state.ak.us/parks

Kenai Fjords National Park
Visitor Center located 1212 4th Avenue, Seward.
Write to: P.O. Box 1727
Seward 99664
907-224-3175
Cabin reservations can be made for the following year anytime after January 2.

Kenai National Wildlife Refuge, U.S. Fish and Wildlife Service
Visitor Center located on Ski Hill Road, in Soldotna.
Write to: P.O. Box 2139
Soldotna 99669
907-262-7021
http://kenai.fws.gov/

Alaska Department of Fish and Game
Area office located at 43961 K-Beach Road, in Soldotna
907-262-9368 in Soldotna
907-235-8191 in Homer
www.state.ak.us/adfg/sportf/region2/r2home.htm
Or, go to the state web site: www.state.ak.us and click on wildlife and fish.

This is an excellent source of information. You can obtain statewide fishing regulations, forecasts, news releases, and even recipes. You can also get your fishing license online.

Other web sites of interest:
Alaska Fly Fishers: www.akflyfishers.org
Alaska Outdoor Journal: www.alaskaoutdoorjournal.com

CHAPTER 2

Why the Fly

Sometimes fate taps you on the shoulder when you least expect it. For me fate came calling in the early months of 1995. A rookie with his name on the Alaska Department of Fish and Game's waiting list, I was hoping for a job, any job, as long as it was outdoors in the country I love. What I got was more than I could have ever, in my wildest dreams, dared imagine.

I was frankly puzzled when the biologist who phoned asked if I liked to fish, if I fly-fished. "Sure," I said, anxious to make a good impression, "I've been fishing all my life." Although I had received my first fly-rod on my tenth birthday, I conveniently left out the fact that fly-fishing remained somewhat of a mystery to me. It was something I saw, quite honestly, as largely a pastime of elitists, having been unfortunate enough to run into that occasional fly-fisher posing as a member of some secret society, making the sport appear more complex and difficult than it actually was.

But the department needed a fly-fisherman to participate in this study, a study to determine the population and age distribution of rainbow trout in one of Alaska's premier streams. If I was hired, it would be my job to help capture, tag, and release these fish.

On the Upper Kenai

Momentarily shocked speechless, I remembered one of those idyllic lakeside afternoons, spent with good friends, when contemplation suddenly turns to whimsy. "The ultimate job"—I remembered one of my buddies saying—"would be getting paid for something you'd do anyway. . . like fishing."

"Not a chance," I scoffed, "not ever."

Yet, as improbable as winning the lottery, here it was—a fisherman's ultimate fantasy. For four months my office would be a drift boat on the upper Kenai River, working a float-only, trophy-rainbow area. My walls would be the majestic snowcapped Kenai Range. My duties would be to explore the many channels of this waterway and all of its rich, jade green holes, every long gravel bar, each with a powerful native 'bow lying in wait. I would be fighting fish that would stir envy in the most seasoned angler. . . and be getting paid to do it!

Needless to say, I lobbied hard for the position, calling back numerous times to reiterate what a conscientious worker I was. Never mind that I was a novice fly-fisherman (that fact didn't surface during my pleading calls) or that, should my efforts be successful, in a few short weeks I'd find myself thrust into the intensity of a painfully brief season during which I'd be expected to learn—and learn fast—the intricacies of a large and very difficult-to-fish river.

But when I finally did land the job, these realities sank in with a vengeance. Fishing, always a relaxing pursuit, had turned into serious business. Suddenly, I found myself under pressure to catch a lot of fish; and I confess that at the outset my rod wasn't exactly hot. Even the guides who helped out on the project, and the volunteers who regularly fished the river, found the spring rainbows difficult. Nevertheless, I took comfort in their assurances, in their absolute guarantee, that as soon as the salmon began their annual migration, dropping eggs as they paraded by and later providing a smorgasbord of decaying flesh as they began to wither and die, right behind them would come voracious trout, turned into feeding machines. "A frenzied attack"—I was promised—"the likes of which you've never seen."

As the river rapidly warmed, sparking a constant increase in emerging insects, the fishing heated up. I learned to ply the waters with stone fly and caddis nymphs, smolt patterns and alevins. And finally, just as my partners had promised, with the return of the salmon the fishing became downright scalding.

My skills grew as well, simply because I was on the river every day witnessing the constant rise and fall of its waters, the creation of new holes and hot spots—all of which an angler would miss if absent even a week or two.

Summer soon fell into place, and with my initial jitters subsiding I began to wonder why it had taken me so long to discover the wonders of the fly. I've always been attracted to activities that put me into the direct flow with nature, that allowed me access to its subtleties and secrets. And nothing, no outdoor pursuit I'd ever known, had drawn me so deeply into this realm—into the domain of the insects, the flow of the water, the run of the salmon, the completion and the start of this entire cycle of life—quite like fly-fishing. For when it's going well, when you allow the river to fill your thoughts, when your rod for a moment becomes like a metronome, keeping time to the music of the trees and to the mysterious beat of the current, it's then that everything insignificant disappears.

With the memory of those slow early days behind me, I had even reached the unprecedented point where, with complete confidence, I began to know where the fish were and what they'd be hitting. In the evenings I found myself wondering not if I'd catch fish, but how many and how large. I'd fall asleep reliving the fights of the previous afternoon, anticipating another day, actually looking forward to the sound of the alarm in the morning and another chance to float beneath eagle nests, to perhaps see a grizzly sow wading with her cubs, to again feel the current of the river pulse up my line, my fly-rod a conductor plugging me into this vital flow of life.

It was about this time my father—an avid fisherman and my mentor—came for a visit from the Lower 48 and was able to volunteer on the project for a few days. I'll never forget picking out a fly I knew was hot, maneuvering the boat over a favorite hole, and then with an uncustomary certainty, directing him to lay his line below a particular riffle—seeing him carefully mend it, then watching his strike indicator dive as if I'd willed it. His customary calm demeanor gave way, his voice rose, and the unmistakable excitement of youth emerged from somewhere deep within him, long buried beneath the layers of his 70-odd years. Those layers shed all at once as he played a 20-inch rainbow to the side of the boat. And then another. And another.

It would be asking far too much to hope that a summer so rich in blessings would include the catch of a lifetime—the one fish that actually takes you away with it as it hammers your fly. A fight that lasts so long time becomes lost, meaningless, as you're transported out of this everyday existence, catapulted into fishing nirvana. Yet that fish did come. Not a rainbow, but an enormous Dolly Varden, on the heel of a near-perfect afternoon—crisp, clear, and windless.

After landing the boat near one of our guide friends and his clients, I decided to walk upstream and work my way back over a nice series of riffles and underwater valleys. At each place I stopped, the water looked better farther along, so I kept walking and eventually found myself around a far bend. Wading out to some decent though fairly fast water, I began to cast, but to no avail. I switched egg patterns several times, working line out almost mechanically, mending each drift without thought as I gazed at the snow- and cloud-capped mountains, tasting greedily the rich essence of pine that spiced the air. No telling how many roll casts I laid out before it happened—before I was startled out of my reverie by that incredible shot. I might have missed a lesser hit, but with the rod nearly wrenched from my hands there was no mistake.

Jolted into action, I instinctively set the hook not once but twice, and then held on, trying my best to slow the sudden departure of line. A salmon, a sea-fresh coho, was my initial guess, because this fish was far too lively to be one of the dying sockeye now littering the stream. Then, just as I regained my wits and a few yards of wayward line, the fish rolled, waving its enormous tail as if taunting me. I knew instantly, felt it in the sudden hollow ache in my stomach, that this was no salmon. Suddenly, all the fish of the past began to filter by in my mind; none compared to this. It was what every fisherman waits for, what I'd been in unwitting search of from the very first time I'd picked up a toy rod and dunked worms for panfish.

More than anything I wanted this one. Wanted to put him into my container, triumphantly carry him back to the boat, and bask in the envious stares of the other fishermen. I wanted to do my duty and tag him, too, but most of all I wanted to document his existence with a photo.

At the moment, however, I had more immediate concerns. I was too far away to call for help, unable to yell above the icy chatter of the river, and the fish seemed to be gaining strength. As he burned into his second charge upriver, and deep into my backing, I realized there was little hope of slowing him down and all I could do was hold on.

Then, abruptly, everything slowed. The usual frantic rush, the fight, fell into slow motion, and I looked around me. A drift boat was passing on the far shore, someone on board involved in a fight of their own, oblivious to mine. They passed beneath an ominous old cottonwood I hadn't noticed before, a craggy, twisted, aged tree wearing an abandoned eagle's nest like a giant crown of thorns. A raven fluttered by, reciting an ancient and mystical chant, while gulls bickered somewhere far overhead.

I don't know how long this went on, a world of thoughts coursing through me as I played this fish near, only to have him set out on another searing run upriver. Finally, after what seemed like hours, with my wrists and forearms numb and my mind still racing, I managed to work him in. Somehow I slipped a net underneath him, and miraculously put an end to our long struggle.

He was everything I had imagined—a huge male Dolly Varden, the finest I'd ever seen, nearly as big around as he was long. I had no idea what his length was, how much he would weigh, and I wanted to find out. But as we paused there, both exhausted, something passed between us. I know that to many a fish is only a fish, but I couldn't do what I'd planned to do. I just couldn't do it. I had too much respect for this fish to force him into the ignominy of a plastic container and carry him off to be ogled by other fishermen.

So, in a dereliction of duty, without taking a measurement or inserting a tag—without even a photograph to commemorate and prove his existence—I lowered the rim of the net and watched him slip away. Afterward, unable to cast, I collapsed on a nearby rock. I sat there for the longest while, recuperating, taking it all in, reminding myself again of how tremendously lucky I was.

Perhaps the only downside to such a job is that it must one day come to an end. For me, however, only the paychecks have stopped. Because now fly-fishing has completely shed its elitist cloak and I am hooked. I must be, because I've carelessly thrown myself into debt for a drift boat and a quiver full of custom rods. And like any addict, or heathen who has recently seen the light, I've begun associating with likeminded, equally obsessed individuals. I now spend my off-season tying flies with The Woolly Buggers, a loose-knit group of the afflicted who while away the winter dreaming, with every new creation, of a certain pool, a particular riffle, and the trout that will rise there come spring. And though I still hold out, waiting for the second phone call—the call that will probably never come—inviting me to once again cast a line for pay, I will continue, like any convert, to sing the praises of the fly to whomever will listen, and to return to the cathedral of the mighty Kenai as often as I can.

PART II

LAKE FISHING

Portaging between lakes

CHAPTER 3

Still-Water Wonderland

At the beginning of the portage I say good-bye to everything above me—the tall trees, the mandarin-hued sky—and beneath the heavy veil of the canoe greet once again the root systems and scattered leaves of the portage trail. I think of the place I am heading, one of my favorite lakes on the Swan Lake system, where I know my fly-rod will soon be swept in its magic arc, the line singing from its reel. I think of my friend Miles, who refused to accompany me here. A die-hard river man, he doesn't believe my tales of 30- and 40-fish afternoons, or that the occasional 20-inch lunker actually lurks here. I think of another friend, Ken, visiting from the Lower 48, who not long ago blithely dismissed my suggestion of a canoe trip. "Well, you see," he said offhandedly, "we have lakes at home." There's just no convincing some people.

The three friends I'm with now needed no convincing, especially my longtime fishing companion, Jim Quinn. Having accompanied me here many times, he knows what the work of portage and paddle will yield. He knows that at the end of a long day we will find ourselves completely alone in a fisherman's paradise.

As we trudge down the trail, Jim's confession, that he's only been

A black bear along the trail

fishing twice this year, still rings in my ears. That admission has brought us here. After years of guiding in bush Alaska, Jim is now in the throes of his first full year in town with a "real" job. It is for his sake we've come. For his sake we've sought out the solitude and renewal that these lakes offer. Here we find ourselves under the spell of nature still raw, cast in the shrill of coyotes and in the haunting echo of the Arctic loon. A spell I hope will be broken only by a spontaneous celebration of our own, the thrilled yelps of that always unexpected moment when the line goes taut.

The portages are flat, and the paddling, despite a slight breeze, is easy. Yet on only our second portage we're stalled by an unforeseen encounter. Nick Esposito, my paddling partner for this trip, has stopped short, so short I nearly ram the upraised canoe into the back of his head. "Bear! Bear," he says haltingly under his breath. From between the gunwales I see patches of brown not 20 yards away. "Let's move back," says Nick, at once both calm and excited. "Okay, but let me turn around," I say, clumsily maneuvering the landlocked canoe around a network of outstretched branches while Nick, stationed between me and the bear, graciously waits—much more graciously than I might have waited had I been in his place.

Retreating with the canoe still over my head, I wonder what to do if the bear follows. Do I drop the boat and find a tree to climb, or do I drop and hide beneath the canoe like a turtle in a Kevlar shell?

But I hear no angry grunting, no snorting, no wild footsteps bearing down on us—just the muffled, measured beat of Nick's pace behind me.

It's not long before we are reunited with Jim and Bill McCrossan, the other half of our party. Neither seems surprised at our hasty return, having heard our false posturing "Hey bear! Hey bear!" all the way back. Nevertheless, we describe to them, in every adrenaline-stoked detail, the 500-pound obstacle standing in our way. Then we inform Bill, the only one with a firearm, that he is to lead. Fortunately, the young grizzly has moved on and we do the same.

By the time we reach our lake and make camp on its lone island, the fickle Alaskan weather gods have turned against us. The storm they've cooked up makes it difficult to hold a canoe in place, let alone cast a line. Soon we are driven from the water and, rather prematurely, into our tents.

I listen as the evening wears on and the foul weather intensifies, rattling the four-season tent unmercifully, berating us in its wet and gusty siege. Awakened during the night by this bleak chorus of wind and driving rain, I think gloomily of the few days we have left before Jim has to return to work. I find it nearly impossible to believe the weather will clear. Yet as I emerge from my nylon hovel in the morning, the wisps of quiet sunshine marbling its walls tell me I have my wish—a dawn in which the clouds have given way to the pale blue of an uncluttered sky and curtains of fog waltz over the mirror of this glorious tree-lined stage, perfectly set and unbroken.

It's difficult to contain my excitement, to stop long enough even for a cup of coffee. Setting out in my canoe, I feel somehow guilty at the intrusion of my paddle into the stillness of the lake, the splintering

A pair of loons

of this unworldly silence by the prow of my boat. Yet there is a warmth to life on a morning like this, a wealth of enchantment cast with each stroke, as I make my way to the far end of the lake, to one of the many "weed forests" that exist a few feet below its surface.

The still water convinces me to try a dry fly. Sometimes, despite a slight chill in the air and the resulting lack of flying insects, these fish can be tempted to the surface. But not today. After trying to coax them with a variety of dries, I give up and dip below the surface with the tried-and-true: a small, black lake leech.

I cast out as far as I can and try to be patient, waiting for the fly to sink. On the first cast I'm too patient and snag. On the second I begin my retrieve earlier, an excruciatingly slow return, with a twitch of the fly here and there, just enough to keep it undulating above the weed beds. It's not long this time before a sharp tug interrupts me and my line snaps to attention. A beautiful rainbow bounds out of the water not 10 feet away. And this one, for the lakes, is big—one of those rare 20-inchers pirouetting wildly around the boat.

While I certainly love the rivers of Alaska, there is something elemental, almost primal, in feeling the full impact of the fish here in calm water. And as I land this first trout of the day, I find myself wishing the others were here to see it, to share the moment with me.

But I do see someone. Jim and Nick, ghostlike through the fog, are working the far shore. Whistling to them and hearing no reply, I get back to business, almost immediately replaying my previous cast—a fish nearly as big, going on a magnificent deepwater run, actually pulling the canoe as it rips line from my reel.

Too excited to respect the silence of the setting, I shout to my friends, finally getting their attention and hailing them my way. Before they arrive I've netted two more fish. Not with fishing prowess, mind you, but simply the luck of time and place. It is a luck we are soon all sharing and that I see painted in particularly broad strokes across Jim's face. And as my friend works his first fish to the side of the boat and holds it up—nearly 18 inches of char, dressed to the nines in the majestic red and gold of its spawning colors—I know it's all been worth it: the long haul in, the bear, and even last night's storm. But more than that I realize these obstacles have not been obstacles at all; they are an integral part of the adventure, part of the beauty of being here.

CHAPTER 4

Approaching a Lake

Approaching a lake in Alaska is not much different than approaching a lake anywhere else. The best time is soon after the ice melts, usually around mid-May, and again in the fall, before freeze-up in mid-October. Be a detective. Look for where fish rest, feed, and migrate. Cover as much area as possible. If the lake is new to you, try trolling in a boat, canoe, or even a float tube. Trail a spinner, spoon, or weighted fly—one with a propeller head, or a favorite streamer—twitching your rod tip or letting line out occasionally while exploring the shoreline.

In contrast to the trout in most rivers, those feeding in lakes move around a lot, constantly on the prowl for food. They are, however, both predator and prey, wanting an easy meal while seeking cover. Look for places that provide both. Overhanging foliage, for instance, furnishes a safe haven as well as a ready food source in the form of insects that live among the leaves and branches and regularly drop into the water. Make note of downed trees, which fish use as migrating paths from deep to shallow water. Prospect around islands, around shoals, and near drop-offs.

Be sure to fish inlets and outlets, where the current stirs up a smor-

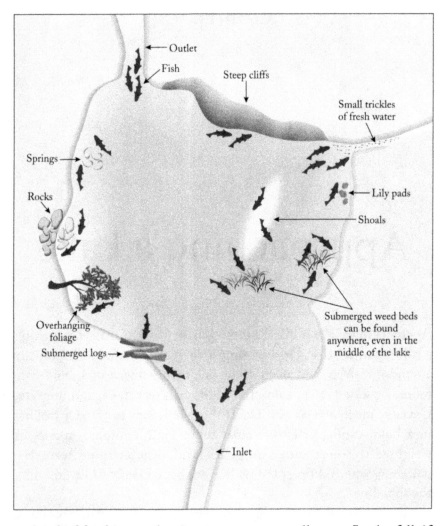

gasbord of food items that in turn attracts small trout. In the fall, if salmon return to the lake, try an egg pattern or Egg-Sucking Leech at any inlet, regardless of how small and insignificant the influx of water initially appears. Salmon have the ability to defy the imagination, spawning in what may look to be no more than a trickle of water, their eggs cascading lakeward, where large rainbows and Dolly Varden are sure to be waiting. Please note that by the time salmon reach this point, they are usually off-limits to fishing. They will have begun to turn crimson and are probably not fit for eating anyway; because of their weakened state, they are also not much sport. Regardless of the regulations it is wise to simply observe them in the lakes and allow them to replenish future generations.

Keep an eye out for small fish on the move, erratically breaking the surface. This is usually indicative of a large fish giving chase, a fish in the middle of a feeding frenzy, an opportunist that will readily strike a fly or spinner cast in its direction. Also be aware of riseforms, the dimples of fish feeding on or near the surface, sometimes barely visible. Try to identify the aquatic insects they may be feeding on. Take notice of the terrestrial or land insects that are around the shore, and always keep a lookout for beetles on lily pads.

Make a mental note, or better yet an actual notation on a map, of the exact location a fish is hooked, and return to this spot. Even better, keep a detailed log not only of where you catch fish but what lure or fly you are using and whether your retrieve is fast or slow. It's also important to keep track of where weeds, drop-offs, and shoals are located.

Unlike rivers, which can be drastically altered by even a slight change in water level, lakes remain relatively constant. And while each one holds its own mysteries, once you uncover the secrets of any given lake—the secret of an obscure weed bed or the migrating path of trout—they are yours forever. The island you fished five or ten years ago, even that patch of weeds, is likely to still be there when you return—and since we never know when that might be, it's always wise to commit those secrets to paper.

CHAPTER 5

Equipment and Tactics

The most useful piece of equipment on Alaska's lakes may be the float tube or canoe. They make fishing much easier, not only because of the thick brush that often fringes the shoreline but because the weed beds where these fish dwell—and, more important, where they feed—are not always found close to shore. They tend to sprout well beyond casting range, sometimes even in the middle of a body of water—often the only fact that differentiates our lakes from many in the Lower 48. Visitors understandably want to ply the shoreline, where fish commonly cruise for food. Many a companion has insisted on fishing a smattering of lily pads, which at first glance seem abundant. But if there's no apparent insect life on the pads, and the lake bottom around them is barren, time will be better spent elsewhere. No one is saying don't hit the shorelines; on the contrary, hit them hard but not exclusively. It's important to keep an open mind. It can be difficult to pull yourself away from where you have been taught to fish, but locating those midlake shoals and underwater weed forests can mean the difference between catching a large number of fish and going home disappointed.

Those not of the fly-fishing persuasion will want to tackle area

Steelhead flies on the Anchor River

lakes with an ultralight spinning outfit, rigged with a quality 6-pound test line. Any variety of small spinners or spoons (⅛ to ¼ ounce) is effective: Krocodiles, Rooster Tails, Super Dupers, Triple Teasers, and, especially, the Mepps Syclops in green or silver. And just because you are using spinning gear, don't be averse to trying a large weighted fly, such as a Woolly Bugger or Egg-Sucking Leech, over the weed beds.

Fly-fishermen will want a 3- or 4-weight rod with a floating line and about 10 feet of tapered leader. If you only have one rod, this allows you, with a split-shot or the addition of a "lead head," to easily switch from dry-fly fishing to wet. However, as dry-fly fishing is an option only about 10 percent of the time, you may want to carry a sink-tip or (especially in the deep lakes) a full sinking line, which is fished with a much shorter leader of approximately 4 feet. This is where more than one rod comes in handy. You never know when one might break, but you also have the luxury of being able to fish either on or below the surface without going through the rigmarole of changing lines.

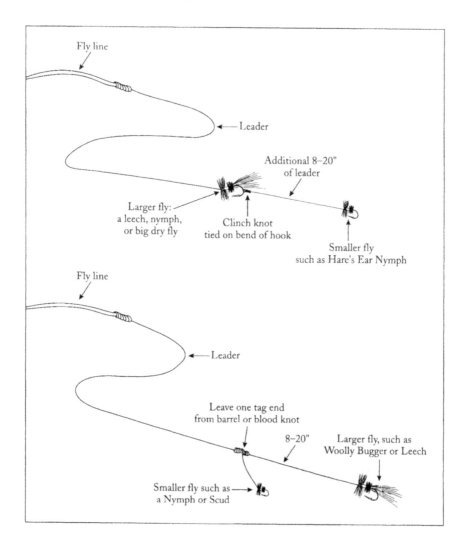

Fly line

Leader

Additional 8–20"
of leader

Larger fly:
a leech, nymph,
or big dry fly

Clinch knot
tied on bend of hook

Smaller fly
such as Hare's Ear Nymph

Fly line

Leader

Leave one tag end
from barrel or blood knot

8–20"

Larger fly, such as
Woolly Bugger or Leech

Smaller fly such as
a Nymph or Scud

Favorite dry flies are the Adams, the black gnat, and the ever-present mosquito, in Numbers 10 to 18. It's also wise to carry mayflies, as well as midges, and various sizes (8 to 18) of the Elk Hair Caddis. Whenever you see beetles on the lily pads around these lakes, try a Crowe Beetle of approximately the same size, often the food of choice of hungry rainbows.

If nothing is rising, go below the surface with your favorite streamer, Woolly Bugger or Woolly Worm. Try Numbers 14 to 20 in a mosquito nymph, or a Hare's Ear of the same size. But do not trek to one of these lakes without a lake leech—a weighted leech pattern tied entirely with black, green, or brown marabou, on a Number 6 to 10 hook. The only trouble with these flies is that, on certain lakes, they're so effective that it's difficult to force yourself to take them off in order to experiment with other patterns.

Whether fishing hardware or flies, it is important to vary your retrieve. Allow your lure or fly to sink to various levels. Count, "One, one thousand; two, one thousand. . ." If you snag, shorten your count. Bring your line in fast, slow, then extremely slow. Try pausing and twitching the rod tip here and there. And, over those weed forests, especially when fishing a nymph, it's that excruciatingly *sloooow* retrieve that will catch the most trout.

You can improve your chances even further by fishing more than one fly, which is legal on most lakes. Try a large dry, such as an Irresistible or a Humpy, followed by a nymph or small leech. The large dry fly works as a strike indicator, but it also keeps the wet fly from becoming snagged on debris. The only way to retrieve this setup is slowly, creeping the dry across the surface. This can also be done with two wet flies: a leech, perhaps, followed by a nymph. As with the previous setup, the second fly, or point fly, should be the smaller of the two. Attach them with an additional 8 to 20 inches of leader, tied to the hook bend of the first fly. Another method is the traditional dropper. Simply tie a barrel knot as you normally would between leader and tippet, leaving one longer-than-usual tag end. In this case the point fly will be the larger of the two (a Woolly Bugger or maybe a leech), and the fly attached to the dropper (a nymph or a small scud) will be the smaller. Fish them slowly and hang on tight; there's the possibility, although rare, of catching two trout at once. If this should happen, you might want to consider purchasing a lottery ticket on your way home.

CHAPTER 6

Finding a Lake

The Swan Lake/Swanson River Canoe System

It's not difficult to find a productive lake on the Kenai Peninsula. Perhaps my favorite locale in all of Southcentral Alaska is the Swan Lake/Swanson River Canoe System. Part of the Kenai National Wildlife Refuge, and connected to civilization only by a narrow braid of dirt road, this angler's paradise encompasses two river systems and more than 70 lakes. It is an area in which the trails and lakes are off-limits to powerboats and landing aircraft. While an inexpensive and relatively accessible destination, it is an area that remains rugged and remote.

You can access this still-water wonderland via the Swanson River Road, at Mile 83.5 of the Sterling Highway. This road snakes through a lush lowland forest of birch and spruce for 17 dust-eating miles before converging with Swan Lake Road, which penetrates an additional 12.5 miles into the heart of the refuge. Stop just about anywhere along these pothole-strewn roads and you will find yourself within a stone's throw of a place to wet a line.

Unfortunately the sad truth in Alaska, like anywhere else, is that the lakes that flank the road system, even a road system as rough as this, re-

Along the Swanson River canoe trail system

ceive a great deal of pressure. Still there are many lakes along this route well worth visiting, especially if you have only an afternoon or two in which to fish.

While it is possible to fish most roadside lakes from shore, the topography makes it worthwhile dragging a float tube or canoe along. Many of these lakes have designated campgrounds along their shorelines; as a rule, these lakes receive the most pressure. Look for those that have no official campsites and require a bit of a walk to reach. Forest Lake, located at Mile 10.5 of Swanson River Road, is a good choice, as is nearby Breeze Lake, at Mile 13.9. Another option is Nest Lake, which can be reached via an easy-to-moderate hike; it begins at Mile 8.1 of Swan Lake Road. Breeze and Nest Lakes are the smallest of the three and are definitely float tube friendly. To reach the farthest shores of Forest Lake, you'll need a canoe.

Another option just off the road is the Drake/Skookum Lakes trail, located at Mile 13 of Swanson River Road. This short trail connects three float tube–sized lakes, passing the lower end of Dabbler Lake, before making a fork: the right side to Skookum Lake and the left to Drake Lake.

Certainly the farther off the beaten track, the better the fishing. Thus an angler with the time and inclination has plenty of incentive to take up the paddle and head into the canoe system for a long weekend, or better yet, a weeklong stay. The system is separated into two areas: the Swan Lake and the Swanson River Routes, each with an incredible number of lakes and a multitude of options for the fly-fisher and spin-caster alike.

The Swan Lake Route

Scenery: 3
Wilderness Experience: 3–5, depending on how deep into the system you go.
Fishing: 4–5
Tip: Fishing improves the deeper you venture into the system. It's best in the spring, after ice-out, around mid-May, or in September, when fall arrives.

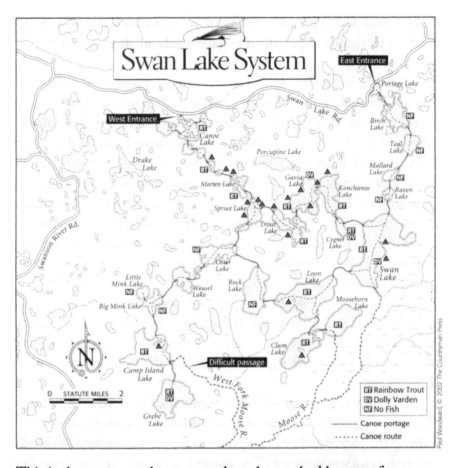

This is the most popular route and can be reached by one of two entrances: the West Entrance at Canoe Lake, Mile 3.9 of Swan Lake Road; or the East Entrance at Portage Lake, Mile 9.7. From either entrance anglers can plan an itinerary that will connect them to as many as 30 lakes, as well as the Moose River. The easiest overnight trip, and the one that puts you quickly into the heart of fishing paradise, starts at the West Entrance. Portage and paddle no farther than Spruce Lake, a trip that can be done at a rather leisurely pace in a couple of hours. The portages to this point are short and relatively flat. There are plenty of good places to camp on either shore, so be kind to the land by picking a site that is already well established. This is also where the fishing really begins to heat up, remaining hot through Trout, Gavia, and Konchanee Lakes. With more time you may want to paddle on to

Swan Lake, which also supports a large population of rainbow and Dolly Varden trout. Swan Lake, being the largest lake in the system, can often get windy and, with so much area to cover, can be difficult to fish. Those budgeting their time may want to paddle on through this lake, passing it up in lieu of some of the smaller lakes in the system, where it's easier to find the shoals and weed forests where these fish hold.

To complete the North Passage, continue from Swan Lake to the East Entrance, where you will need to leave a second car. The Kenai National Wildlife Refuge estimates this circuit to take two to three days, in anyone's estimation a rather relaxed canoe trip. However, if you want to spend more time with a rod in your hands than a paddle, consider adding an additional day to your trip, or returning the way you came, via the West Entrance. While it's natural to want to charge ahead and see new scenery, backtracking may be warranted in this case, considering the four lakes that lie between Swan Lake and the East Entrance (Raven, Mallard, Teal, and Birch Lakes) have no fish.

If you're interested in a little longer trip, you may opt for the Central Passage. Back at Spruce Lake, simply point your canoe south and follow the trail system to Loon Lake. The portages, while remaining well marked and fairly flat, do get considerably longer at this point. But there's ample reason to keep up the pace and not linger at either Otter or Rock Lake because both are devoid of fish.

Its easy access and good fishing make this route nearly as popular as the North Passage. So, unless you are traveling in the early spring or late fall, you are apt to have plenty of company, even midweek. To avoid some of the traffic, fishers may want to take a detour at Loon Lake. From here, you can access Clam and Moosehorn Lakes, which have no viable outlet and are often bypassed by visitors just out for a camping trip. All three lakes have excellent rainbow fishing and hold some very large trout.

From Loon Lake it's on to Swan Lake and the East Entrance, or a trip down the Moose River. The Moose River is flat-water paddling with the likelihood of a few beaver dams to cross. The trip takes a full day (two would be better) and entails leaving a second vehicle at Izaak

Walton State Recreation Area, in the town of Sterling.

For those of a more adventurous nature, and with more time on their hands, there's the West Passage. From Otter Lake follow a series of small lakes into Camp Island Lake. This is definitely a step farther into the wilderness. The trails from this point are not as well defined nor as clearly marked, and it takes an extremely long, rather strenuous day to reach the lake.

There are several points to consider when making a trip to Camp Island Lake. First, there are no fish along the way, and the lake itself, while full of sizable rainbow and char, is large, deep, and subject to a great deal of wind—making it, at times, difficult to fish. There's only one decent place to make camp, and that's on the lake's namesake, its lone island, which at the height of summer or during moose season is often taken. Second, you must take into account the long journey out. The most likely route, down the west fork of the Moose River, can be difficult, especially when the water is low. This very narrow, serpentine stream has dozens of beaver dams to cross.

Lakes in the Swan Lake System that do not contain fish include Big Mink, Birch, Mallard, Otter, Raven, and Teal.

The Swanson River Route

Scenery: 3
Wilderness Experience: 3–5
Fishing: 4.5
Tip: Fishing is best in spring or fall. Look for underwater weed forests. Try a Syclops or lake leech over weeds, and vary your retrieve.

This route covers 60 miles, linking more than 40 lakes with the 46-mile-long Swanson River. As a result of longer portages, and the extra time and physical effort required to explore it, this route sees considerably less traffic than the Swan Lake Route. From the entrance at Paddle Lake (Mile 12.6 of Swan Lake Road), the intrepid paddler has the option of heading to Gene Lake by either the east or west route. This is by far the most accessible part of the system and the most popular.

A typical Swan Lake/Swanson River rainbow

The journey to Gene Lake can be undertaken in a single day. Although with the fishing stoking up almost immediately on entering the system, there's simply no need to push it. Make camp along the way and enjoy what nature has to offer. If you take the western route, one option is to pitch your tent on the island at Campers Lake or along the shores of Swanson Lake. There are not as many campsites on Swanson, but the fishing on both the northern and southern ends of the lake is excellent.

From here it's a short hop to Gene Lake, and easy access to Pepper Lake. Gene Lake has an island in its northwest corner where you can camp. Around this island you will find some of the best fishing this system has to offer, although all of these bodies of water have prominent shoals and those ever-present patches of weeds that begin to bloom in early summer. Fish around these shoals and weed forests for rainbows and char that regularly reach 17 and 18 inches in length and occasionally even surpass that 20-inch threshold.

If you opt for the eastern route out of the system—via Woods, Red

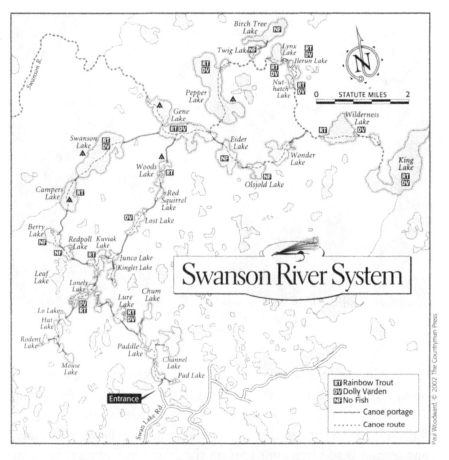

Swanson River System

RT Rainbow Trout
DV Dolly Varden
NF No Fish
.... Canoe portage
· · · · · · · Canoe route

Squirrel, and Lost Lakes—plan on leaving early or camping along the way. The fishing in this series of small lakes is top-notch. If you're leaving Gene Lake via the Swanson River, be prepared. Although most maps show this route as entirely a water passage, the first 1.5 miles is a portage over a crisscrossing bramble of beaver dams and log-jams. Once on the upper Swanson, this narrow, flat-water stream meanders 19 miles to the first take-out at Swanson River Landing, at the end of Swanson River Road. If the water is low, as it often is in mid-summer, the first 2 miles of paddling can be difficult. A few weeks without rain can turn a pleasant float into a grueling slog through what is essentially a lily pad–choked quagmire. The marshy terrain can also make campsites along the river difficult to locate. Look for sites on rises at river bends and on the surrounding hills. The positive aspect

Casting a line on a calm day

of taking the river home is the fishing. Even though the trout, as a rule, are not quite as large as those in the lakes, most times of the year they will readily rise for dry flies, making this an excellent choice for the fly-fishing purist with a taste for adventure. To find out more about the Swanson River, including how to access its lower reaches, please turn to chapter 14, "The Quiet Alternative."

Only those in the mood for a true wilderness endeavor will want to venture east of Pepper Lake. The going from here can be challenging as a result of the extensive wetlands that are often too deep to portage yet too shallow to paddle. This is especially true from Nuthatch Lake to Wilderness Lake, where waders are required to amble your boat 1.5 miles through an old weed-glutted streambed. The route from Gene Lake, via Eider Lake, is just as difficult. And while it's a good idea to have a basic knowledge of the map and compass anywhere on the system, here it is essential. This trip should be undertaken only by those who have extensive orienteering skills, a great deal of energy, and an open-ended schedule. Adventurous fishermen take note: If you have gone to all the trouble to venture to this far-flung corner of the Refuge hoping for complete isolation and solitude, you may be disappointed. Several years ago outfitters were given permission to fly into King and Wilderness Lakes, which in all practicality is the terminus of this route. If you're interested in a fly-in trip, you may want to check with Refuge Headquarters to see who currently holds the contract for these lakes. A drop-off to either lake is an excellent way for those who don't have the time, or who are unable to handle the rigors of an extensive backcountry trip, to experience the incredible fishing the Refuge has to offer.

Dauntless souls making the canoe trip, who crave solitude, may want to fish Lynx, Ilerun, and Nuthatch Lakes. The only lakes with fish along the way, and too small to land a plane on, they are likely to be completely uninhabited—by humans, that is.

Lakes in the Swanson River System that have no fish include Berry, Birch Tree, Eider, Olsjold, Redpole, and Twig.

Resurrection Pass Trail
(Trout, Juneau, Swan, Devil's Pass Lakes)

Scenery: 4
Wilderness Experience: 2.5
Fishing: 2

This trail begins in Cooper Landing, at Mile 53 of the Sterling Highway. First used by miners in the late 1800s, now it is extremely popular with hikers and mountain bikers. Expect to be sharing the trail with large groups from June through early September. Part of Chugach National Forest, the route winds its way through the Kenai Mountains to its terminus at the small mining town of Hope, on Turnagain Arm. The first lake, Trout Lake, is a 3.5-mile hike from Cooper Landing. This lake has stocked rainbow trout and a few lake trout, which are best pursued in the early spring or the late fall. For those lucky enough to have a reservation with the Forest Service, there is a public-use cabin and small rowboat provided for the occupant's use.

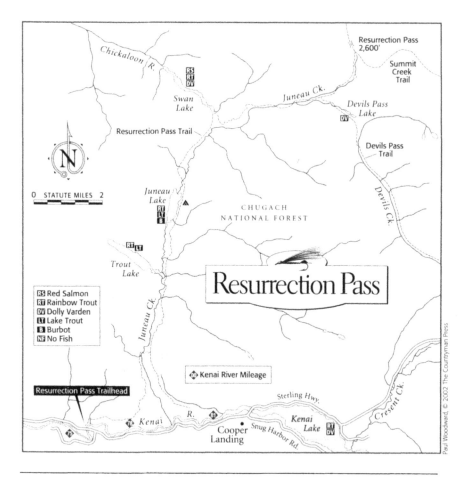

Juneau Lake

Scenery: 5
Wilderness Experience: 2.5
Fishing: 3

Next along the trail is Juneau Lake, 6 miles above the Sterling Highway. There are two Forest Service cabins located along its shores, each with a small boat available. Juneau Lake is a fairly large body of water, with stunning views, and a healthy population of rainbow trout, lake trout, and burbot. This is the only lake on the peninsula with burbot, a freshwater member of the cod family. Fish for them deep with a jig or with any variety of bait.

Swan Lake

Scenery: 5
Wilderness Experience: 2.5; 5 on the west end of the lake.
Fishing: 3.5
Tip: The best fishing is on the west end of the lake. Try an Egg-Sucking Leech deep.

Swan Lake is 9 miles from the Cooper Landing trailhead. It has Forest Service cabins located on either end of the lake. The east cabin lies along the trail; the cabin on the west end is accessible only by float-plane. There are large numbers of rainbow trout, lake trout, and Dolly Varden present here. The best fishing can be found on the west end, in the fall, when red salmon make their way into the lake via the Chickaloon River. At this time of the year, fish egg patterns or Egg-Sucking Leeches at the outlet or along any of the small inlets along the lake's steep shoreline. On all three of these lakes you will want to allow ample time for your spinner, spoon, or fly to submerge, and this is where fly-rodders may want to employ a full sinking line.

Devil's Pass Lake

Scenery: 5
Wilderness Experience: 3.5
Fishing: 2

The last lake along this route is Devil's Pass Lake, 13 miles from Cooper Landing, or accessible via the Devil's Pass Trail (an arduous climb of 4 or 5 hours), which begins at Mile 39 of the Seward Highway. Although this lake receives very little fishing pressure because of its remote location, and has a decent population of Dolly Varden, the fish tend to run relatively small by Alaskan standards, making Devil's Pass a good place for light tackle.

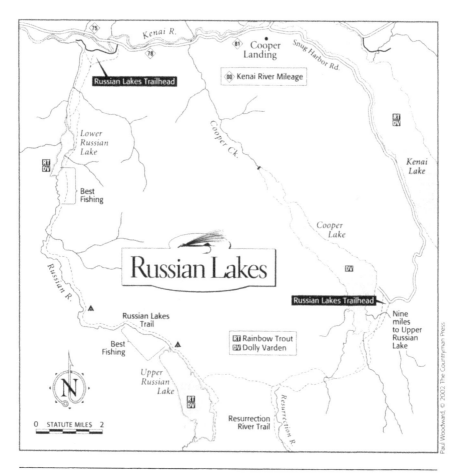

Russian Lakes Trail
(Lower Russian Lake)

Scenery: 5
Wilderness Experience: 2
Fishing: 2
Tip: Fish the inlet or outlet at either end of lake. Best in late summer, early fall.

There are two lakes in this system. Lower Russian Lake is an easy 2.5-mile hike, along a handicap-accessible trail that begins within the boundary of the Russian River Campground. This popular campground is located at Mile 53 of the Sterling Highway. The Forest Service cabin at Lower Russian Lake features ramps at the doors and on

Lower Russian Lake

the dock for wheelchair users. This lake is a good family destination because of the easy trail. It does receive a great deal of fishing pressure during the summer, making these fish somewhat of a challenge. Please note that the lake is closed to the taking of salmon because it is a spawning area. The best fishing for rainbow trout and Dollies is in the fall at the outlet, near the mouth of the lower Russian River, or at the inlet at the southern end of the lake. Heavy brush and berry bushes make the inlet difficult to reach as well as prime bear habitat. You can fish with any variety of small spinners or spoons. Fly-fish with egg patterns and Egg-Sucking Leeches in the fall. Try streamers, Woolly Buggers, and nymphs throughout the year.

Russian Lakes Trail
(Upper Russian Lake)

Scenery: 5
Wilderness Experience: 4
Fishing: 4.5

The Forest Service cabin on Upper Russian Lake

Upper Russian Lake is a 12-mile hike from the trailhead at Russian River Campground, or a 9-mile trip from a trailhead at the end of Snug Harbor Road, which runs along the west shore of Kenai Lake. The turnoff for this road is at Mile 48 of the Sterling Highway. Either of these popular trails takes you a step deeper into the Alaskan backcountry and into prime bear habitat. The trails also lead to some marvelous fishing. These trails are excellent for mountain biking, but those more interested in fishing than biking or hiking may want to consider one of the many floatplane services that fly into these lakes.

The Forest Service cabin on this lake is a true Alaskan gem: an old log cabin, originally used by trappers. There is even a creek running nearby to serenade tired fisherman to sleep. The best part about having the cabin, however, may be the boat that comes with it. Because of the lake's size, having a boat exponentially increases the options for fishing. The cabin's popularity, however, means that reservations need to be made well in advance. There is also excellent camping on the northern end of the lake. Many anglers who fly in

On the trail to Upper Russian Lake

bring along an inflatable boat or float tube, if they don't have the cabin. Those who have the cabin may want to consider flying in a small motor for the boat.

Fishing on this lake can run from good to phenomenal. It is closed to salmon fishing, but the rainbow trout can reach and even occasionally surpass the 20-inch mark. Use the same flies as on Lower Russian Lake and fish deep at the outlet, near the mouth of the upper Russian River. A slow retrieve with a black or purple Egg-Sucking Leech can be deadly. In the fall try a simple egg pattern or glo bug with white rubber legs, fished deep at any inlet. I discovered this fly by mistake. Recently transplanted from back East, I happened to have a red bass popper with legs, and for some unexplained reason I tied it to the end of my line, sinking it with a large piece of lead. The trout loved it. I never forgot. After several years of living in Alaska, I tied a series of red and pink glo bugs with white legs and fished them anywhere there was water flowing into this lake. They haven't worked as well anywhere else, but here the results have been nearly miraculous. Perhaps the legs look like a piece of the egg sack, or more likely, they resemble some type of insect common to Upper Russian Lake, an insect that feeds on salmon eggs. Whatever it is, it works when the salmon are in and laying eggs.

Spin-casters can easily fish any fly by either keeping it suspended off the bottom with a bobber, or by using only a little bit of weight, and retrieving it very slowly. Those using spinning gear will also want to try a yellow Rooster Tail.

Johnson Pass Trail
Johnson Lake and Bench Lake

Scenery: 5
Wilderness Experience: 3.5
Fishing: 3.5
Tip: On a calm night try dry flies for rainbow trout on Johnson Lake and grayling on Bench Lake. If the fish aren't rising, go below the surface with a nymph or your favorite spinner.

This trail is part of the original Iditarod trail, and if you look closely you can find a few artifacts and the remains of old cabins, now overrun by vegetation. The trail begins at Milepost 63.8 of the Seward Highway and runs 23 miles to its southern terminus at Milepost 32.5, near the Trail Lakes Hatchery. The best bet is to bring a partner and leave a car at either end of the trail. The entire route can be traveled by mountain bike in a single day, but that leaves little time to fish. A better idea is to make a weekend out of it. There are excellent campsites on the southern end of Johnson Lake, which lies approximately 10 miles from the northern trailhead. Because these lakes are above the tree line, firewood is scarce; you may want to bring a small camp stove.

Johnson Lake has a decent population of rainbow trout; the best fishing is near the outlet on the southern end of the lake. Try dry flies here on a calm evening, and if fish aren't rising, try a small Hare's Ear nymph. Or cast your favorite spinner at any of the lake's inlets or outlets.

The next day you can head to Bench Lake, which lies about a

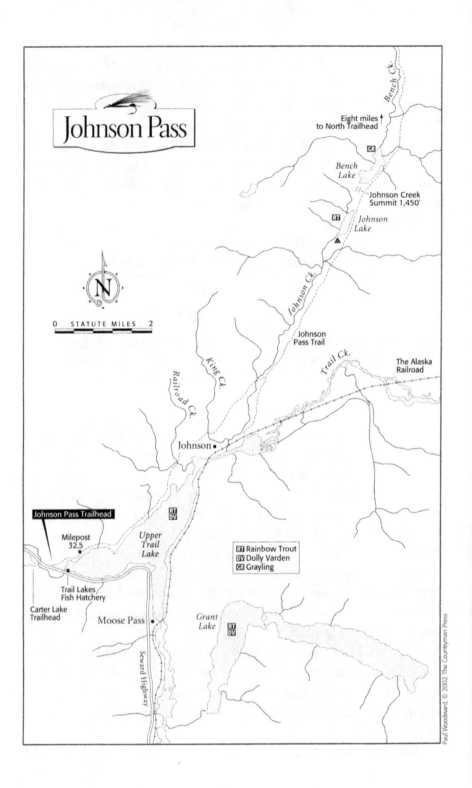

Johnson Pass

Bench Ck.

Eight miles
to North Trailhead

GR

Bench
Lake

Johnson Creek
Summit 1,450'

RT Johnson
Lake

N

0   STATUTE MILES   2

Johnson Ck.

Johnson
Pass Trail

Trail Ck.

The Alaska
Railroad

Railroad Ck.

King Ck.

Johnson •

Johnson Pass Trailhead

Milepost
32.5

Upper
Trail
Lake

RT
DV

RT Rainbow Trout
DV Dolly Varden
GR Grayling

Trail Lakes
Fish Hatchery

Carter Lake
Trailhead

Moose Pass •

Grant
Lake

RT
DV

Seward Highway

Paul Woodward, © 2002 The Countryman Press

mile to the north. Here you will find grayling, which are most easily taken on dry flies but will also hit any variety of small lures. For more on grayling, please turn to chapter 7.

Going for Grayling

Along one of the many switchbacks of the trail, I stop pedaling and wait for my beating heart to catch up. My breath sends plumes of mist rising upward, fogging my glasses and reminding me of just how steep the first 2 miles of this trail are. I'm barely into the journey and already it's obvious from the throbbing in my legs and the pain rising in my derriere that I haven't been riding much this year. As I dismount my bicycle—which is suffering from a bit of disrepair, having spent the better part of the summer corralled in the garage—I begin to wonder what's become of my friend, Richard. Like me, Richard is an avid fly-fisherman but a rather reluctant mountain biker. I also find myself wondering, as the pain in my chest begins to subside, if this is such a good idea.

That's about the time I hear a noise behind me. A sudden procession of spandex-clad cyclists, barely breaking stride, pump by at what to me is a rather ridiculous pace. As they pass, I can't help feeling even more inadequate as a mountain biker. I have none of the accoutrements of the sport—no special shock absorbers, no biking gloves, no toe clips—and there's a Pepsi can sticking out of the rack where a water bottle belongs. But unlike these pursuers of the sport, I won't be just turning around and going home when I reach the end of the trail. I wish they'd slow down, so I could explain to them the true importance of the bicycle. It's so much more than a mere recreational vehicle. To me it's an important tool, a means to an end—an easier way to reach Crescent Lake and to be quickly engaged in the joys of fishing. But I just give them a gracious nod as they pass in their ignorance. I must admit, just for a moment, I'm unable to help feeling slightly superior.

Then, taking up the rear, in stark contrast, comes Richard. Dressed in baggy clothes, and saddled with waders and with rod tubes bungeed to his bike, he doesn't fit in with the rest of the throng as he cycles toward me and then dismounts.

"Let's go," I say, "we need to keep up with the crowd."

"Yeah, right," he says between deep gasps. "They'll probably be on their way back down before we even break out of the trees."

But we're not going to let this bother us. Not with a trace of autumn just beginning to permeate the air, and with wisps of sunlight finally penetrating the overhanging spruce. We know we are in the right place. It won't be long now before things flatten out and we emerge from the darkness of the forest into a sweeping alpine meadow. A meadow of fireweed and wildflowers, clouds draped around the surrounding mountains—a truly staggering view, a scene that conjures up memories of Julie Andrews prancing through the Alps, or in this case pedaling her Cannondale.

Of course, at the conclusion of this breathtaking jaunt, we will also be exposed to one of Alaska's most pleasant surprises—grayling, daintily sipping our dry flies off the surface. This small, exotic, and abundant salmonid, known for its large, kite-like dorsal fin, will not only allow us an escape from the maddening crowd, it will offer a welcome change of pace from bouncing heavily weighted egg patterns in big water. It is an opportunity to break out the 4-weight fly-rods. And by riding, despite our rather dubious skills as bicyclists, we will be able to turn this into a day trip, an hour and a half to ride the 6.5 miles in, and a mere 45 minutes careening our way back out. Our only regret is that we don't have more time to take advantage of the lake's Forest Service

Richard Kelso, riding to Crescent Lake

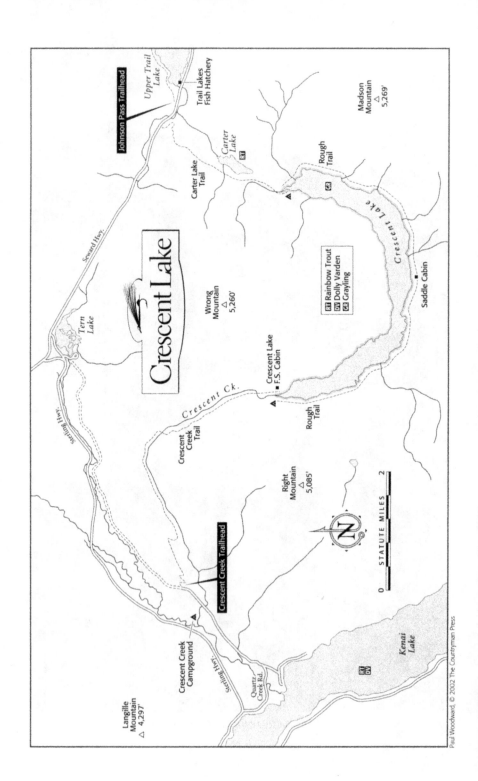

Crescent Lake

Johnson Pass Trailhead

Upper Trail Lake

Trail Lakes Fish Hatchery

Carter Lake

Carter Lake Trail

Madson Mountain △ 5,269'

Rough Trail

Seward Hwy.

Tern Lake

Wrong Mountain △ 5,260'

	Rainbow Trout
	Dolly Varden
	Grayling

Crescent Lake

Saddle Cabin

Crescent Lake F.S. Cabin

Crescent Ck.

Crescent Creek Trail

Rough Trail

Sterling Hwy.

Right Mountain △ 5,085'

N

0   STATUTE MILES   2

Crescent Creek Trailhead

Crescent Creek Campground

Langille Mountain △ 4,297'

Sterling Hwy.

Quartz Creek Rd.

Kenai Lake

Paul Woodward, © 2002 The Countryman Press

Float tubing on the east end of Crescent Lake

cabin and the boat that goes along with it. We do know, however, that if the wind stays down we will have plenty of action from shore—unbeatable action, and on the surface.

Crescent Lake

Scenery: 5
Wilderness Experience: 3.5
Fishing: 4.5
Tip: Try dry flies on either end of the lake.

Crescent Lake is accessible by floatplane or by the trail located at the end of Quartz Creek Road, which branches off the Sterling Highway at Milepost 45. This 6.5-mile-long trail quickly climbs into alpine country and features one of two Forest Service cabins located on the lake. The other cabin lies another couple of miles down the south shore and is best accessed by air, because the trail that continues along this side of the lake can be marginal due to winter avalanches and falling rocks. A few moments before reaching the lake you will pass Crescent Creek, which also holds many grayling and is a good alternative if the lake is windy. Please note that as a result of late spawning, fishing in both the lake and the creek does not open until July 1.

Another way to access Crescent Lake is via the Carter Lake Trail, a moderate hike of about 3 miles, which originates at Milepost 33 of the Seward Highway. This trail at midpoint passes its namesake Carter Lake, which is stocked with rainbow trout. Because the beginning of this trail is so steep, mountain biking is not recommended. The trail, however, is cut wide, which makes it easy to carry in a float tube. Although there are no cabins located on this end of Crescent Lake, there are several excellent campsites and the same spectacular views.

Grayling in general are not finicky and will rise for most dry flies—Griffith's Gnat, Black Gnat, Mosquito, Adams, and Royal Wulff included. Occasionally the wind will rise on Crescent Lake, making fishing difficult. This may be the time to go below the surface with streamers, Woolly Buggers, or Muddler Minnows. Anytime is a good time for spin-casters to fish small spinners or spoons. Try a silver Vibrax or Super Duper, or the always deadly green Mepps Syclops. The grayling taken out of this lake are the biggest you will find on the Kenai Peninsula, many reaching the 17- to 19-inch range.

Lower Fuller Lake

Scenery: 5
Wilderness Experience: 3
Fishing: 4.5
Tip: Bring a float tube and light gear, and fish dry flies over the weeds on the north end of the lake.

Lower Fuller Lake can be reached via a short, well-marked trail at Milepost 57 of the Sterling Highway. It ascends quickly and offers excellent views of the Kenai Range and Skilak Lake. Although this steep, rather strenuous 2-mile hike negates the use of most watercraft, a float tube is well worth the effort. The fish along the edges of the lake run small, while the larger fish (13–15 inches) tend to hold in the

A float tube trip to Lower Fuller Lake

deeper water, over the weed beds that seem to abound on the north end of the lake. Here, as in Crescent Lake, dry-fly fishing is the most productive method. Try any type of dry fly, including those mentioned for Crescent Lake. If you are fishing hardware, vary your retrieve; be careful to retain a tight line and not snag in the weeds.

Grayling Lake

Scenery: 3.5
Wilderness Experience: 2
Fishing: 2

The easiest hike for grayling on the peninsula, this lake lies a mile down the trail that begins at Milepost 124 of the Seward Highway. A good family trail and an excellent float-tube lake, it does receive a lot of pressure because of its location.

Grayling

Paradise Lakes

Scenery: 5
Wilderness Experience: 5
Fishing: 5
Tip: The fish are small, so bring the lightest gear possible.

Lower and Upper Paradise Lakes are aptly named. Nestled deep within the Paradise Valley and accessible only by air, they represent the paradise we all picture when contemplating fishing in Alaska: a secluded lake with a panorama of magnificent scenery, and a multitude of hungry fish vying for our attention. The grayling in both lakes do run small, in the 10- to 13-inch range, but are abundant. Lower Paradise Lake has the added bonus of a small number of rainbow trout. Be sure to come armed with your most ultralight spinning outfit or a 2- or 3-weight fly-rod.

Only a 10-minute flight out of the town of Seward, these lakes provide an excellent weekend escape and are a relatively inexpensive option for those looking to get away from it all. Both have Forest Service cabins and boats. Here some advance planning is required. For instance, reservations for cabins need to be coordinated with those for air travel. But it is well worth the effort. These are lakes you are likely to have all to yourself, where it's not uncommon to hear the drone of a wolf or to see a family of bears meandering across one of the many patches of white that grace these magnificent windswept mountains. Start with standard grayling tackle, but bring a wide range of lures and flies, because after 50 or 100 fish it's fun to experiment, to see what these fish *won't* take. Shop around for the best airfares and make cabin reservations through the Forest Service.

CHAPTER 8

Lakes along the Road System

Lakes along the Road System

Scenery: 2–5
Wilderness Experience: 1
Fishing: 1–3

Most of these lakes receive a great deal of pressure and patience is often required when fishing them. That does not mean, however, that they should be overlooked. At certain times of the day or year, they can come alive and provide some excellent action.

Heading South from Anchorage

Summit Lakes

You'll find the Summit Lakes at Mileposts 46 and 47 of the Seward Highway. The upper lake has a Forest Service campground and parking

Float tubing one of the many lakes along the road system

area on the lake's eastern shore. Both lakes have many small Dolly Varden, with a few in the 14- to 16-inch range. The larger fish tend to run deep and can most easily be caught by bait fishermen using salmon eggs. If you have access to a boat, you may want to troll the shorelines with your favorite spinner or spoon. Fly-fishermen will have the best luck early or late in the year, fishing either end of the lake with the usual selection of dry flies, nymphs, and streamers. Try smolt imitations in the spring.

Jerome Lake

Located at Mile 38.5 of the Seward Highway, Jerome is a shallow lake with rainbows and Dolly Varden. Fish from the bank or inflate your float tube and cast near the outlet at the southern end of the lake. Because of its proximity to the highway and large parking lot, Jerome Lake is an easy place to launch a small car-top boat. These fish will hit the usual flies and lures, but in midsummer, your best bets are shrimp or salmon eggs.

Tern Lake

This lake is located at the junction of the Seward and Sterling Highways, commonly known as the "Y." It is a shallow, weedy lake that contains a very small number of Dolly Varden. A few of these fish, however, migrate in from the Kenai River and do run large. Tern Lake is better known for bird-watching than for fishing.

Upper and Lower Trail Lakes

These lakes run from Mile 32 to Mile 25.5 of the Seward Highway, above and below the town of Moose Pass. They contain lake trout, rainbow trout, and Dolly Varden. Anglers can fish from the banks, spincast, and troll on these lakes. The southern end of Lower Trail Lake is a popular place to soak bait (herring or salmon eggs) for lake trout.

Vagt Lake

Park at the south end of Lower Trail Lake and follow the trail for a mile, along the southeastern shore and into the nearby countryside. There are stocked rainbow trout—a few have grown very large—but they run deep. Allow ample time for your lure to sink. Fly-fishers will want to employ a sink tip or a full sinking line. The fishing is not hot, but the view at this quiet, picturesque lake is well worth the walk. It's a great place to have a picnic with the family.

Grouse Lake

Grouse Lake is a very small lake, 7 miles north of the city of Seward, at Milepost 120. There is limited parking, and this lake receives a great deal of pressure. The best fishing is in the fall for Dolly Varden.

Heading West on the Sterling Highway

Jean Lake

Jean Lake has a small campground and runs parallel to the Sterling Highway, starting at Mile 60. It is a fair fishery for small rainbow trout and Dolly Varden. Fish either end of the lake, near its inlets and outlets.

Hidden Lake

Take a detour at Milepost 58 of the Sterling Highway. Follow Skilak Lake Road for 3 miles, to Hidden Lake Campground, where there are well-developed tent and RV sites and a boat launch. This lake contains rainbow trout and Dolly Varden but may be the best opportunity anywhere on the peninsula for anglers to catch lake trout. Lakers will cruise the shallows soon after ice-out or in the late fall. This is a good time for fly-fishers to get on the water and cast streamers, such as a Mickey Finn, or to trail any shade of leech from their canoe. Fishing will be best early in the morning or at dusk. Through the summer months or at midday, boaters fishing for lake trout will want to fish the deeper water with jigs or with bait. There is the added bonus on this lake of kokanee (land-locked red salmon) that run in the 14-inch range. Boaters need to exercise caution as the winds can rise here without warning and are occasionally funneled across the lake through a narrow valley.

Ohmer Lakes

These two small lakes are located at Mile 7 and Mile 8 of Skilak Lake Road. The lower lake has a small campground. Both lakes contain rainbow trout and Dolly Varden.

Engineer Lake

Located at Milepost 9.5 of Skilak Lake Road, this lake contains rainbows, Dollies, and landlocked silver salmon that run up to 16 inches in length. There is a small camping area and ample parking.

Pack, Marsh, and Bottenintnen Lakes all lie along Skilak Lake Road and are devoid of fish.

Kelly and Peterson Lakes

A turnoff at Milepost 68 of the Sterling Highway and a short drive will deliver you to either of these popular lakes. Both have camping areas and gravel boat launches, and both contain rainbow trout.

Egumen Lake

Park at the Egumen Lake Wayside, at Milepost 70, and follow this heavily trodden trail for about a mile. If you are feeling particularly strong, this is a good place to carry in a canoe; if it is calm, try a float tube. This lake contains rainbow trout, which on a quiet evening will rise for dry flies. Try to match the hatch; in this area it's often mosquitoes.

Watson Lake

Turn at Milepost 71 of the Sterling Highway and drive a quarter mile to the lake. There you will find a small campground and a decent boat launch. Despite its popularity, Watson Lake is an excellent early season and fall rainbow fishery. Although it is connected to two other lakes (Alfonasi and Imeri), the best fishing is on Watson Lake, not far from the boat launch, where the east fork of the Moose River exits the lake. There are many nice weed beds. Try trolling around them with a Mepps Syclops or casting on their edges with a small plug. This is also a good place to cast a dry fly on a calm night.

North Kenai Road

Mile 1 of this road actually begins at the turnoff of the Spur Highway in Soldotna. Take this road north, through the city of Kenai, and follow the signs toward Captain Cook Recreation Area. The majority of the lakes along this route are on private land, although some have public access sites.

Cabin Lake

Turn at Mile 21.5 of the North Road and follow Miller Loop Road for 2.5 miles. There is a small parking area and decent fishing for rainbow trout. Fish the usual flies and spinners, and use salmon roe during the height of summer.

Daniels Lake

There is a small parking area at Mile 30 of the North Road. This lake has rainbow trout and Dolly Varden, but it does receive a great deal of fishing pressure.

Stormy Lake

Part of Captain Cook Recreation Area, this lake has a campground, swimming area, and boat launch. There is good fishing, especially in the fall, for rainbows and char around the many weed beds. This is an excellent spot to troll a leech pattern or streamer behind a canoe.

Stocked Lakes

The Alaska Department of Fish and Game has a stocking program on various lakes throughout the Kenai Peninsula, including Scout Lake, at Milepost 85, and Arc Lake, at Milepost 100, of the Sterling Highway. Johnson Lake and Centennial Lake, on Tustumena Road (the turnoff is at Milepost 111 of the Sterling Highway) are also part of the program. These lakes are stocked with either rainbow trout or landlocked silver salmon, which generally reach 12 to 14 inches in length, and can be excellent sport on light tackle.

For a complete listing of lakes currently being stocked, contact the Alaska Department of Fish and Game in Soldotna.

Part III

RIVERS AND STREAMS

CHAPTER 9

One More Try

The water dripping off the eaves has thickened into crystal stalactites and a heavy frost has bloomed overnight as snowflakes swirl with fallen leaves in a welcome prelude to winter. Still, I'm not ready to give in, to succumb to the torpor of dark days, to hunker down indoors tying flies and watching videos of Floridians catching strange fish.

So I'll call my friend, Richard Kelso, and we'll begin our usual end-of-season refrain, reminding each other how cold it is and that the gear is all put away. A verbal tango we go through every year that will end when one of us suggests we give it one more try.

That's usually all it takes before we find ourselves chopping ice out of the bottom of the drift boat and heading to the upper Kenai River, passing trailers loaded with snow machines and car tops framed in skis and snowboards.

At the launch site the few motorists who pass seem to feel a need to honk as if in recognition of our insanity, or perhaps in an effort to share it.

"That's right, we're crazy," acknowledges Richard, as he and our friend Jerry McDonnell struggle into enough neoprene, polarfleece, and wool to insulate an Everest mountaineer.

An icy day along the Anchor River

And Richard is right. You'd have to be at least somewhat off-kilter to even consider fishing on a day like this, when the guides of your rod are destined to ice up time and again. When the mere thought of plucking a fly out of the box and tying it on is painful. And when fishing is sure to be interrupted by several long walks or by that peculiar fisherman's jig that's performed only along frozen streambanks, that rite of autumn designed to jump-start circulation and warm blood-depleted extremities.

But there are reasons that inspire our madness. Perhaps it's the sense of urgency, of adventure, that comes to life in extreme weather, even in a place you know well. Maybe it's fisherman's intuition, whispering that, as the mercury begins to climb even a little bit after the overnight freeze, the trout will become active and begin feeding. Perhaps most telling is the fact that we know there will be no other fishermen, only eagles, to compete with.

It's as if we've been transported 50 or 100 years back in time. Every hole is ours for the taking. A hush has fallen over the entire stream. In fact, even the most heated war zones in the summer battle for sockeyes have returned to the spirit of the river. Now only bear tracks, and salmon carcasses left by fallen water, mire the shoreline.

If we had opted for the streams of the southern peninsula, for Deep Creek or the Anchor River, we would have been much less likely to find this kind of solitude. Despite the fact that they will be pounded by the elements, or forced to cast between chunks of ice, die-hard anglers are lured here by the score. The prospect of tangling with a steelhead is enough to drive the most lethargic, the most unenterprising fisherman, from the warmth of his lair and convince him to give it just one more try.

Certainly my own thoughts, along with the steelhead, return to those streams each year. For it was on them that Richard and I first learned the art of pushing the season. We'd been coaxed out of autumnal lethargy by our good friend Tony Lewis, who had reiterated what we'd been hearing for years: Of all the fish celebrated in fly-fishing mystery and lore, the steelhead is the ultimate. This proved to be a truth that I would be long in verifying.

Though the steelhead streams were not far from my home, they were new water to me and carried all the mysteries and challenges of such. The eyes of fishermen I'd never seen before turned on me as if I'd just stumbled into their favorite small-town watering hole. The techniques I observed were as strange and as varied as the people I saw employing them: the fly-fishing purist, casting and mending a light line, stood next to the sneaker-clad spin-caster lobbing an enormous burden of lead down the middle of the run.

But despite feeling a little lost and out of place, I quickly settled in, hardly aware that this was the beginning of an odyssey that would encompass the next several seasons. Soon I was devoting every winter to reading about these fish and every fall to watching, studying, and imitating technique, and experiencing the joy and frustration of watching my friends land their first, second, and third fish. My will to continue was bolstered only by the occasional flirtation with success: the soft touch of a steelhead, the flash of its profile in the current, its occasional brief show of strength at the end of my line.

A Kenai River rainbow

My patience was finally rewarded on a rainy, windswept November afternoon. At long last I was able to correctly incorporate a few of the techniques I had seen with my own intuition and timing. Then, finally, I experienced the almost inconceivable power a steelhead displays as it bolts upstream, melting line from the reel in unimagined fury.

But the upper Kenai River, where we're headed today, holds its own rewards, not the least of which are its large native rainbow trout, many approaching the size and strength of their sea-run cousins.

The water this time of year is low and forces us to undertake the arduous task of hauling the boat over a maze of emerging gravel bars. But despite the required effort, Richard likes it better this way. It's more like fishing one of those steelhead streams, he says, than a large river. Unlike steelhead, however, which hang like torpedoes in the cold, fast runs, the trout that remain in the Kenai this late tend to hold in slow, deep pockets, and these pockets become more pronounced and easier to read as the river recedes.

By the time we reach the second such hole, the walls of cloud have lifted. All that is left of the snowflakes is a wonderland of dust-laden banks and frosted trees. And the sun, at last cresting above the mountaintops, suddenly feels much warmer than the 30 degrees it officially bestows upon us.

Jerry, first out of the boat, moves into place with the determination and single-mindedness of an athlete lining up for a big race. Skunked our last time out, he quickly positions himself where the gravel ends and a riffle skirts the abyss of slow water, vowing retribution with a sparse purple Egg-Sucking Leech. This fly, he assures us, will succeed when all else fails.

Sure enough, his offering barely has a chance to sink before the dull, muted rhythms of impending winter are interrupted by something spectacular. Fireworks burst at the surface of the pool. Scales merge into a mosaic of black dots and a swirl of pink. Jerry's reel sings with redemption.

And in the intervening moments, amidst the sudden sweet panic of playing a large fish, time rushes to a standstill. Numb fingers and cold feet are forgotten. Each one of his senses, every aspect of his being, is tied for an instant to the river through this fish. A fish Jerry will continue to play, bringing it near enough to leave the blush of its gill plates, the silver pleated curve of its shape, embedded in the current of his memory.

And for seasons to come, as those around us forsake their fly-rods for a shotgun or deer rifle—or a good book in front of the fire—such images will keep us coming back. Giving it just one more try. And when the river is too low to float and the launch sites are piled high with snow, we will walk to our favorite holes and hot spots, huddled in a weight of winter clothes and staring at the ice-bound waters, and we will be warmed by our memories.

CHAPTER 10

Approaching a River

Rarely if ever will you see old-timers simply plunge into the water without a plan, without stopping to study the river in which they are about to cast. At other times, seemingly without warrant or warning, they pick up and move to another spot that for some inexplicable reason looks good to them. To the uninitiated, or to those new to a particular stream or type of fishing, this behavior may seem akin to some mysterious sixth sense—it may even have evolved into this—but it originally began as simply the ability to read the water. This reading of the water is a language that, for many of us, at first appears to be written in a foreign tongue. But this is a language we can learn. And if we use it enough, it will soon become like second nature, a part of our own intuition and timing, until we find ourselves regularly thinking like fish—yes, like fish.

To begin reading a river, we want to construct a picture, a mental image, of what lies both above and below the surface. The first step is to stop and survey the situation. In general, fish in rivers are the same opportunists they are anywhere else. They want to expend the least amount of energy possible while being able to feed at will. They also want to stay out of danger's way. They will seek the safe haven of over-

A nice one on the Upper Russian River

hanging banks, downed trees, and deep water. Of course, fish behavior varies by species. For instance, when salmon enter fresh water, they become more interested in spawning than feeding. Often on their long journey to natal streams, they seek out pockets of slow water—places to rest rather than places to find food. Trout and Dolly Varden, on the other hand, are solely interested in finding a meal, and they need the current to deliver it to them. They will leave safe water to feed, but ideally they are looking for a place where the drift will bring them a steady supply of terrestrial and aquatic insects, small fish, and salmon eggs. At the same time they do not want to fight the current. A classic example is behind a rock, where the flow is broken. But look for any such breaks in the current, including completely submerged rocks, downed trees, gravel bars, back eddies, and abrupt bends in the river. Fish hang along these current lines or "seams." A seam can also be formed where two currents of differing speeds meet, where a tributary enters a stream, or below an island.

Some of the largest fish tend to hold in deep pools. These sanctuaries, carved out by years of river flow, often form below a series of riffles or at the base of submerged gravel bars. Here there is a sense of cover, the water is well oxygenated, and there is a steady supply of food being continually washed into the pool. Everything a fish wants.

Be careful, however. It's not uncommon for anglers to wade through some very fishy water when they see one of these pools, or a likely looking gravel bar, beyond casting range. Do not fall into this trap. Always start casting close and work your way out. Appearances can be deceiving. The contour of the river bottom—even in fast, shallow, and choppy water—will often allow fish a holding place. Even big fish will venture into these riffles if there are salmon eggs or insects being filtered through. Often these fish, willing to vacate their usual sphere of comfort, are actively feeding; but because they don't have any cover, they are also the most skittish. You will need to practice some stealth as you wade.

Rivers are forever changing. Yesterday's hot spot can be today's dead zone, especially in large rivers like the Kenai. A sunny or cold spell, or a few rainy days, can cause the river level to rise or fall drasti-

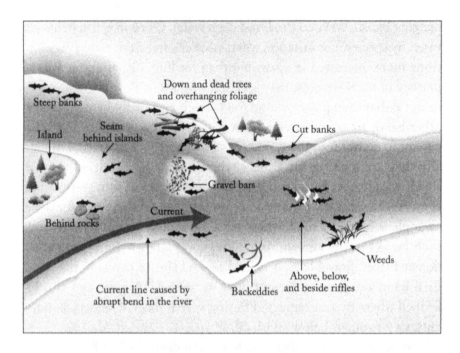

Down and dead trees and overhanging foliage

Steep banks

Island

Seam behind islands

Cut banks

Gravel bars

Behind rocks

Current

Weeds

Current line caused by abrupt bend in the river

Backeddies

Above, below, and beside riffles

cally. So even on waters you know well, it's important to stop and contemplate what the river is telling you. Look not only for obstructions like logjams and gravel bars; notice what's actually in the water and how it's getting there. Are insects, for instance, falling from overhanging vegetation, and where are they going once they hit the water? Are they being slapped into the main current, pushed into an eddy, or funneled into a quiet run? Are there hiding places nearby, a weed patch or a cut-bank under which a fish can find refuge?

A great deal of planning goes into fishing Alaska's streams. The equipment and techniques you use will vary depending on the time of year or the type of water you are planning to fish. It will also depend on which species you are targeting, a difficult decision with salmon, steelhead, rainbow trout, and Dolly Varden—all worthy objectives. Because so much depends on timing, place, and species, we will try to pinpoint techniques and equipment throughout this section, as they pertain to certain rivers and fish.

Regardless of where you choose to go, or which species you are aiming for, attempt to view the river in parts *and* as a whole, deciding what you'd do, where you'd go, if you were the fish. Do this enough and you will find you are learning a new language, reading the river, and eventually, just like the old-timers, developing that fishy sixth sense.

CHAPTER 11

The Kenai River

Kenai River

King Salmon: First run May to early June. Second run early July to season closure, usually July 31.
Red Salmon: First run May to mid-June. Second run Mid-July to late August.
Silver Salmon: First run July to mid-August. Second run early September to season closure, usually September 30.
Pink Salmon: July to mid-August.
Rainbow Trout and Dolly Varden: Season usually opens June 11, in most parts of the river, with fishing picking up throughout the summer and peaking in September.
Tip: Because of its size, if you are able to fish the Kenai River only once or twice a season, or a lifetime, consider hiring a guide.

There's no doubt—the Kenai River is Alaska's most famous fishery. The destination of thousands of visitors every season, it is widely profiled both in print and on television. Too often, however, jubilation turns to disappointment when a visiting angler is confronted by this large and often intimidating piece of water or by the crowds that con-

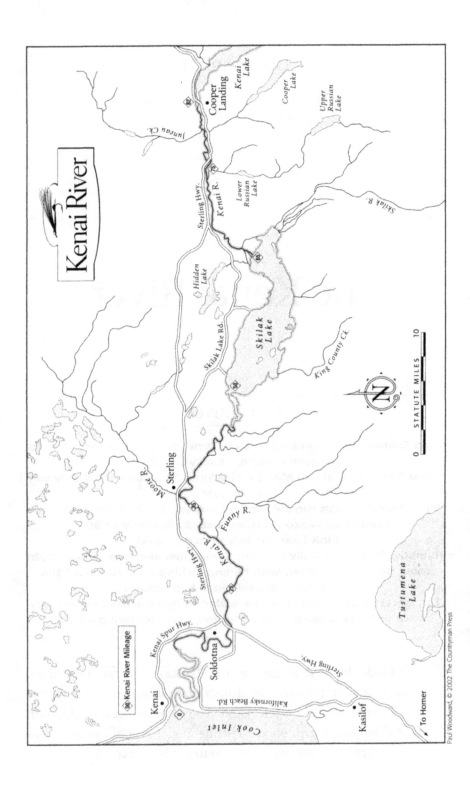

Kenai River

gregate in certain areas along its banks. That is a shame, because the closer you get to this river, to its rippling pools and turquoise water, the more it seems to infiltrate your head and heart, with each visit placing you further under its spell, enticing you to return again and again.

Carving its way for 80 miles through a patchwork of diverse environs, the Kenai River might better be viewed not as a single river but as many rivers. Its drift-only area, for instance, a renowned trout fishery flowing in braids through the Kenai National Wildlife Refuge near Cooper Landing, is a world away from the river's lower reaches, where powerboats vie for position in the annual bid for king salmon.

There are areas of the river that are accessible only by boat and others that can easily be reached on foot. There are famous combat zones, where the salmon are usually plentiful and you are sure to find yourself shoulder to shoulder with other anglers. And there are trout holes, where you are just as likely to find yourself alone. But whatever your tastes, it is a river that truly has something for everyone. The Kenai may be the best opportunity, especially for those on a budget, to tangle with a king or coho salmon, to fill a cooler with hard-fought sockeyes, or to experience the thrill of playing a large native rainbow trout, a descendant of the same fish that occupied these waters thousands of years ago.

Upper Kenai River

Scenery: 5
Wilderness Experience: 2.5

For our purposes we will divide the river into three parts: upper, middle, and lower. The upper river flows out of Kenai Lake, beneath a bridge at Milepost 48 of the Sterling Highway. It works its way through Cooper Landing and down the Kenai River Canyon, 17 miles to its terminus at Skilak Lake. Much of this area is designated drift-only, making it closed to powerboats. It is also catch-and-release only for rainbow trout. Though it is a Mecca for fly-rodders casting for

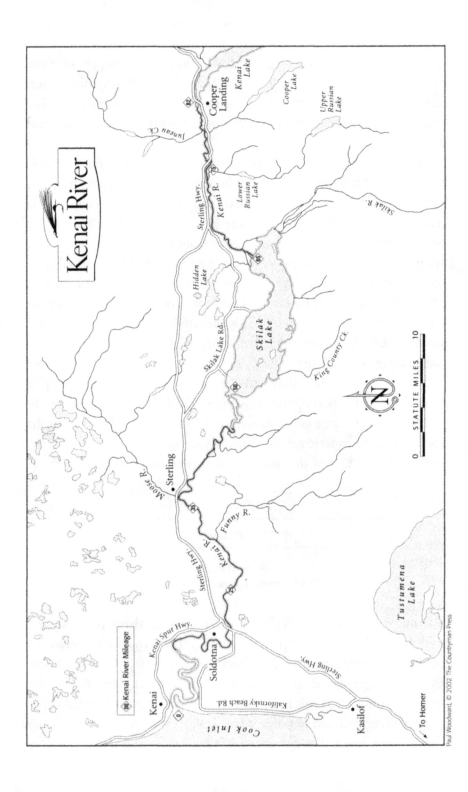

Kenai River

Cooper Landing

Kenai Lake

Cooper Lake

Upper Russian Lake

Juneau Ck.

Sterling Hwy.

Kenai R.

Lower Russian Lake

Skilak R.

Hidden Lake

Skilak Lake Rd.

Skilak Lake

King County Ck.

Moose R.

Sterling

Funny R.

Kenai R.

Sterling Hwy.

Kenai Spur Hwy.

Soldotna

Tustumena Lake

Kenai

Kalifornsky Beach Rd.

Sterling Hwy.

Cook Inlet

Kasilof

To Homer

Kenai River Mileage

N

STATUTE MILES

0   10

Paul Woodward, © 2002 The Countryman Press

The Upper Kenai

these world-class rainbows, it is also well known for its salmon fishing. In fact, Alaska's most famous, perhaps infamous, combat zone—the confluence of the Kenai and Russian Rivers—is in this section. It is strictly a sockeye and silver salmon fishery. Because so few kings make it to this part of the river, there is no open season for them.

Middle Kenai River

Scenery: 4.5
Wilderness Experience: 2

The middle section of the river could itself be divided in two. Its upper portion begins at Skilak Lake and flows for 11 miles to Bing's Landing, a state recreation site near the town of Sterling. This part of the river is accessible mainly by boat. It is a popular area for all salmon fishing, including kings. It also holds some excellent trout water; for

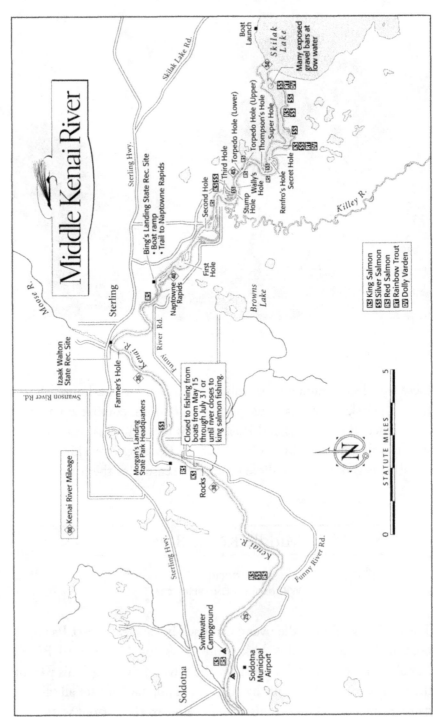

Middle Kenai River

Moose R.

Sterling

Skilak Lake Rd.

Sterling Hwy.

Bing's Landing State Rec. Site
• Boat ramp
• Trail to Naptowne Rapids

Boat
Launch

Skilak
Lake

Many exposed
gravel bars at
low water

30

Second Hole

Third Hole

Torpedo Hole (Lower)

Torpedo Hole (Upper)
Thompson's Hole
Super Hole

45

Stump
Hole

Wally's
Hole

Renfro's Hole

Secret Hole

Killey R.

First
Hole

40

Naptowne
Rapids

Browns
Lake

River Rd.

Funny River Rd.

Izaak Walton
State Rec. Site

Farmer's Hole

35

Kenai R.

Swanson River Rd.

Morgan's Landing
State Park Headquarters

Closed to fishing from
boats from May 15
through July 31 or
until river closes to
king salmon fishing.

Kenai R.

Rocks

30

Kenai River Mileage

00

Swiftwater
Campground

Soldotna

Soldotna Municipal
Airport

35

Funny River Rd.

Kenai R.

N

STATUTE MILES

0   5

KS King Salmon
SS Silver Salmon
RS Red Salmon
RT Rainbow Trout
DV Dolly Varden

Paul Woodward, © 2002 The Countryman Press

fly-fishers this is especially true in autumn when the water begins to drop. Biologists with the Alaska Department of Fish and Game report that in the fall months, the largest congregation of fish anywhere on the Kenai Peninsula may be here, in the first few miles below Skilak Lake. A few remaining sockeye salmon and newly arrived silvers gather in this area, attracting large numbers of rainbow trout and Dolly Varden; and even lake trout are moving into this part of the river to spawn.

The middle section of the river continues on from Bing's Landing another 20 miles to the city of Soldotna. From this point the river begins to widen substantially and the current becomes swift, making trout fishing difficult. This stretch of the river is mainly fished by boaters searching for salmon, although there are also many popular access points for those wishing to fish from shore.

Swift currents, submerged rocks, and shifting gravel bars characterize this entire section of the river. Numerous guide services operate within this area; but if you decide to take your own boat, it's important to know how to operate it under these conditions. You need to know the basics of running a river, including how to read the current and how to avoid the many obstacles typically found in a waterway of this size.

Lower Kenai River

Scenery: 2.5
Wilderness experience: 1

What is commonly referred to as the lower river begins at the Sterling Highway Bridge, in the city of Soldotna. From here the river flows for 21 miles before reaching its terminus in Cook Inlet. It is in this section that the majority of Kenai River kings are taken. And when the fish are in, the lower Kenai is also typically where the largest congregations of fishermen can be found. While most king salmon are taken from boats, there are numerous opportunities for those on foot to fish for sockeye, silver, and pink salmon. Public access sites are sprinkled throughout this section of the river, but because of its proximity to civ-

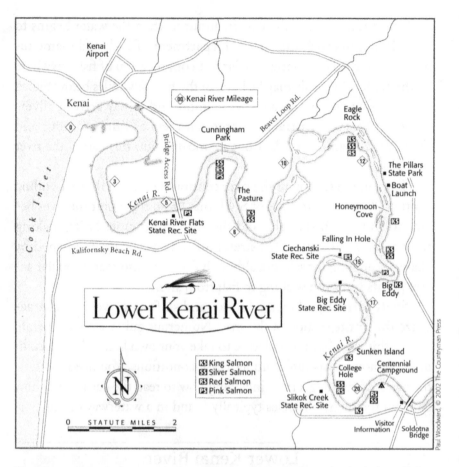

ilization, you can expect a lot of company during the height of the season.

While the current in this portion of the river tends to be slightly slower, there are still some difficult sections, and boat handlers would be well advised to have experience in navigating inland waterways. It is especially important here, because of the increased boat traffic, to be well aware of the "rules of the road" and to be courteous to your fellow operators.

Kenai River Rainbow Trout and Dolly Varden

Opening day in mid-June heralds another season of trout fishing on the Kenai, which immediately brings to mind the upper river. With its braided channels, long gravel bars, and deep rich pools, this is the type of water trout devotees salivate over. And spin-casters need not feel left out. In fact, at the start of the season, before salmon begin dropping their annual banquet of fresh eggs, the most effective means of catching trout, and that most commonly employed by guides, is the pulling of plugs; that is, holding a single-hook Hot Shot or Wiggle Wort in the current. This technique is usually undertaken with a medium-action spinning rod while keeping a boat anchored, or paddling, above a likely looking hole. Later in the season, spin-casters will turn to flies. To do this they will use a sinker commonly referred to as a slinky. These sinkers are available at most tackle shops, or you can easily make one by stuffing parachute cord with metal shot and using a cigarette lighter to seal the ends. The slinky is then attached to the line with a snap swivel and cast upstream, the fly trailing it by a leader length of 18 to 24 inches. This rig can be fished from shore or trailed along behind a drifting boat. Either way you will want just enough weight to feel it tapping along the bottom—too much and you will get snagged, not enough and you will miss the fish. It is vital that the weight is ticking, tapping, and meandering around rocks, but it is also extremely difficult for a newcomer to differentiate between the way this feels and a strike. Try not to be overeager, but if you're in doubt, set the hook.

Unfortunately for fly-fishermen, the Kenai is probably not the river of choice for the dry-fly aficionado. The silt carried from distant glaciers, which gives the water its unique jade green hue, can also leave the river somewhat cloudy. Also, because of the river's speed and size, and the type of food usually available, most of the rainbow trout and Dolly Varden remain below the surface to feed. Thus the most common technique for catching these fish with a fly-rod is dead drifting, the same technique that is used in most parts of the country to fish nymphs. In Alaska dead drifting is also used to present egg patterns and the ever-popular flesh fly, a fly used to mimic the decaying flesh of salmon that have died in the river. Most fly-fishers use a 6-weight rod with floating, weight-forward line. Many anglers up the size of their line to a 7- or 8-weight to get more distance out of their

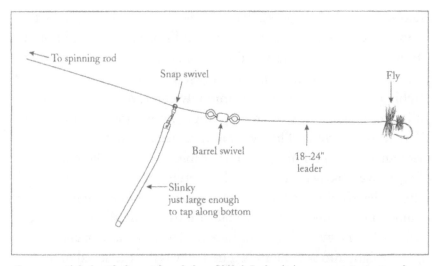

In areas with deep holes, such as below Skilak Lake, it is common to motor above a particular hole and drift this rig through it. This is also a common technique for King fishing on the Middle and Lower Kenai River. For Kings a larger "slinky" is used and the fly is replaced by a Spin-N-Glo and salmon eggs.

cast, which can be important on a river of this size. Typically the setup for dead drifting consists of a 10-foot leader with a strike indicator attached near the fly line, and a small split-shot or twist-on sinker about 20 inches above the fly. You will want the least amount of weight possible, while still keeping the fly on the bottom of the river. It's imperative, especially with egg patterns and flesh flies, to keep the fly deep.

Cast directly upstream or up-and-across, which is most easily accomplished using a roll cast. Curt Muse, owner of Alaska Troutfitters, one of the premier guide services on the upper Kenai, has developed many innovative techniques for roll casting, as well as a system for dead drifting downstream of the angler. His method of dead drifting includes what he refers to as an extended loop. As with most nymphing techniques, it is important to mend your line in order to maintain a drag-free drift. However, with the extended loop you will want to mend downstream as the fly approaches, allowing your line to form a U (a downstream loop) about 2 feet wide and 2 feet directly below your strike indicator. Although this is something fly-fishers are taught not to do, from this point it is possible to feed all the line you

A king salmon caught backtrolling on the Lower Kenai River

Dead drifting in the dead of winter

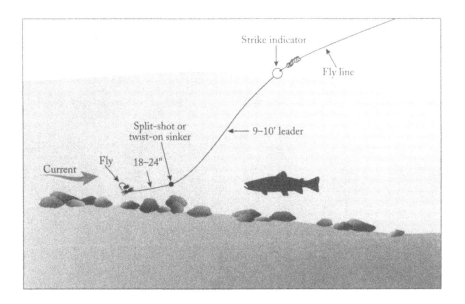

want into the loop. The technique requires a bit of practice to perfect, but amazingly enough the indicator, and more important, the fly floats naturally on its way, allowing the angler an extremely long downstream drift and more opportunity to entice a fish. With this downstream loop it is important, however, to keep your rod low and to set your hook back rather than up. This is because the excess line on the water does not allow for a quick hook-set when raising your fly-rod. By striking low and back upstream, the line will be pulled through the water and instantly come up tight on the fly and the fish. It sounds easy, but anyone who has fished for a while may find it difficult to set a hook this way. Raising your rod is an instinct that is extremely difficult to break.

When dead drifting, presentation is everything, which means a drag-free drift. Shunned by many as simply a bobber, the strike indicator may be your most useful tool when it comes to maintaining a good drift in big water. Not only does it allow you to detect more strikes and detect them quicker (essential when finicky fish are barely tapping your fly), but it also serves as a vital information link to what is going on below the surface. In other words, if your indicator is not behaving itself, neither is your fly; if one is dragging, so is the other. More than merely a bobber, a strike indicator is also a drift indicator,

DENNIS REAGAN

The author holds a Kenai River Dolly Varden

instructing you on presentation, telling you when to mend your line. It's also common on big water to use a brightly colored, hard-foam indicator to keep better tabs on your drift. Many also use a bright-colored fly line to help them.

If you are not catching fish dead drifting, it is probably because of one, or a combination, of these four reasons: (1) Your fly is not getting to where the fish are. Add or subtract some weight. (2) Your presentation is off. The fly is dragging and doesn't look natural, so mend the line accordingly. (3) You have the wrong fly. Try another color or change to something else. (4) There are no fish in this spot. Because the water level may have changed, no food is being filtered into this particular hole and the fish have moved. Time for you to move on, too.

Remember that on the Kenai River, larger water means larger gear. When you attempt to dead drift on smaller streams, be sure to downsize everything so you don't scare the fish. In shallow, clear water you will need a very light strike indicator—many use a feather or piece of yarn, or nothing at all, allowing their floating fly line to serve as the indicator. You will need a lighter, tapered leader, and you will have to be much more conscious of where you are casting. You don't want your fly, indicator, or line spooking the fish. You may also want to use a shorter line method of dead drifting, which basically entails moving the indicator down your leader in conjunction with the depth of the stream—about double the water depth above the fly. In general, you use a shorter cast with this method and mend your line upstream as you would if fishing a dry fly, avoiding drag at all costs. Under certain circumstances you may also want to use the strike indicator to keep a nymph suspended in the water column, where emerging insects are often found during a hatch.

As stated before, a river—especially a river as large and dynamic as the Kenai—is forever changing. Water levels are constantly rising and falling, week by week, day by day, minute by minute—any time of year. Unfortunately, fishing every day is a luxury most of us don't have. The harsh reality is that if you are gone for even a week or two, you may find yourself back at ground zero, hunting for today's favorite hole or hot spot. Still, there are some things you can count on.

The annual die-off red salmon supplies food for the entire river, especially trout.

The river will close from May 1 until mid-June to protect spawning trout, and just prior to this closure you will want to fish nymph patterns. The rainbow trout during this period are extremely selective; it will be necessary to search the water, and perhaps even run a screen through it, to find out what type of pattern to try. There are caddis flies, stone flies, and mayflies present in Alaska, so have a wide range of nymphs available. Try any color of Hare's Ear, from cream to green. Have Pheasant Tail and Prince Nymphs, with or without a bead head. You may have to switch flies often, but if you find the right nymph, watch out—fishing this time of year can be incredible.

When the river opens back up in June, continue with nymphs, but also try dead drifting an alevin pattern, which is meant to imitate the newly hatched salmon fry. This is also the time of year that smolt (juvenile salmon) may be migrating out to sea. There are many smolt patterns available, and they should be fished in typical streamer fashion, with a short leader, quartering downstream-and-across. Sculpins and Muddler Minnows can also be fished this way and are extremely effective, especially at the edges of deep pools. Fish them with a fast sink-tip line, stripping them back in, and always varying your retrieve.

When the salmon begin appearing in earnest, usually early to mid-July, it is time for the spin-caster to switch from pulling plugs, and the fly-fisher to switch from nymphs and streamers, to egg patterns—if not the rainbow's favorite food, certainly the Dolly Varden's. In the not-too-distant past egg patterns consisted of glo bugs, tied with yarn or chenille, but in recent years they have largely been replaced by hard plastic beads that are threaded on the line, usually above a bare hook.

It's true that a lot of fly-fishers find the use of egg patterns in general, and beads in particular, distasteful. The fish, however, do not. While many anglers deny that this is even fly-fishing, there is simply no denying the effectiveness of a glo bug or bead cast below spawning salmon. Simply dead drift them as you would a nymph, making sure they remain very close to the bottom of the river.

Despite what has been written and said of eggs, slight color changes do make a big difference. With the first sockeye, try a flame red glo bug or bead, and fade to pink or nearly white as the season progresses. Try dimming beads by painting them with a pearl or frost nail polish.

With the die-off of the first-run sockeyes, break out the flesh flies. Made from rabbit strips or glo-bug yarn, these flies, as their name implies, are designed to imitate the flesh of decomposing salmon. Start off with any combination of mottled red, pink, or white, and go to brown and completely white by fall. Try an "egg-sucking flesh fly," a flesh fly with a pink, orange, or red egghead. You can actually find these at most fly shops on the peninsula.

When the air gets cold and early-season frost begins to bloom, there is no reason to stop fishing. Along with your polypropylene underwear and polarfleece, all you need is a bit of patience and a good attitude. By late fall and early winter many of the resident trout have headed to the nearby lakes, and those that remain tend to be less active. Often the fly needs to be placed right in front of their noses in order to entice them. Still, fishing this time of year can be quite productive, and there is a very good chance you will have the river all to yourself.

If you are fishing late into the season, and there hasn't been a high-water event to wash salmon carcasses away, immediately go to a flesh fly. If you don't find any carcasses, or if the flesh patterns fail to produce, go back to a sculpin, Egg-Sucking Leech, or Muddler Minnow.

Accessing the River

There are many ways to reach the upper Kenai on foot. Some of the easiest access and best trout fishing can be found from Milepost 55 to Milepost 58 of the Sterling Highway. There are numerous pulloffs and heavily trodden trails that lead to the river on the south side of the highway. Just below the Russian River, if not too glutted with salmon fishermen, is an excellent place to cast for rainbows and Dollies as well. The Kenai River Trail (a 4.5-mile round trip), accessed by two well-marked trailheads on Skilak Lake Road, brings fishermen into the Kenai River Canyon. Hidden Creek Trail, at Milepost 4.5 of

Skilak Lake Road, will deposit anglers on the shores of Skilak Lake and they can hike south to the mouth of the river. This is about a 4-mile round trip, and an excellent early- and late-season fishery. It is a certainty, however, that on both trails there will be plenty of bear signs, both scat and tracks, and a good possibility of seeing a bruin.

The time frame and general recommendations for trout fishing on the upper river hold true for the middle river as well. For those with a boat, fishing trout below Skilak Lake can be phenomenal, although fly-fishers may have the most fun in the fall when the water begins to recede. That's when, especially in the first few miles below the lake, long gravel bars become exposed and deep pools are more readily accessed with fly gear. This area of the river is known for its many deep pockets of water, which are more conveniently fished with conventional equipment. You will have the best luck by either casting or pulling plugs, or by motoring above these holes and drifting through, using the "slinky-fly" method described in the diagram on page 114. You can fish this method with a fly or, if you're not having any luck, try replacing it with a small plug.

Anyone can learn to fish the Kenai River. If, however, you are able to fish it only once or twice a season, or a lifetime, it might be worth seriously considering the services of a guide. Remember to shop around, and always get references.

Please note that below Skilak Lake anglers are currently allowed to keep one rainbow trout and two Dollies (of various sizes) per day. With salmon being monitored very closely, and usually having very generous bag limits, there is simply no reason to keep a rainbow trout or Dolly Varden. These are true native fish—trout whose ancestors lived in these waters thousands upon thousands of years ago—and there are very few like them left in the world. If you catch a trophy, consider a plastic mount. They look just as good, last longer than a stuffed fish, and can be made from a photograph. Be careful while handling the fish, quickly take its picture, and please, let it go. That way future generations of anglers will be able to enjoy these fish for a long time to come.

Salmon Throughout the System

The Kenai River is home to four of Alaska's five Pacific salmon. Each shares many traits in common. They are anadromous, meaning they divide their lives between fresh and salt water, and are migratory, that mysterious inner clock steering them back to their natal streams after significant time at sea. Yet each kind has its own defining characteristics in size and color, in how it grows and feeds, and even how it behaves on the end of a line.

One thing is for certain: Salmon runs are unpredictable, and the timing of runs can only be estimated. Despite the best efforts of agencies like the Department of Fish and Game, there is simply no guarantee whether a run will be weak or strong, or on time. Avoid disappointment by having a backup arrangement; never plan a trip solely on fishing for salmon.

It's also worth noting that all salmon upon returning to spawn in fresh water begin to deteriorate, losing their bright silver sheen. It's when they metamorphose, turning a deep mottled olive, maroon, or crimson, depending upon the species, that they become less sporting to catch, losing much of their fight. They are also not nearly as good table-fare; their meat deteriorates along with their outside appearance.

Chinook or King Salmon

Blue-gray back with silvery sides. Small, irregularly shaped black spots on back, dorsal fin, and usually on both lobes of the tail.

Spawning king salmon adults lose their silvery bright color and take on a maroon to olive-brown color.

There is a reason the chinook, the state fish of Alaska, is also called the king salmon. It is usually differentiated from other salmon solely on the basis of size. Characterized by its blue-gray back and the small black spots on its sides and tail, the king is North America's largest, and perhaps most sought after, freshwater sport fish. Kings can easily reach 50 or 60 pounds in the Kenai River, waters that also boast the world's largest sport-caught king, a 97-pounder, landed in 1985.

It's no wonder anglers flock here every year to fish for these behemoths—and fish they do. The Alaska Department of Fish and Game estimates that on average it requires 20 hours of unguided fishing, and 12 hours of guided fishing, to land a king. Of course this is an average, a combination of those storybook days at the peak of the run and those long hours of prospecting before the fish show.

Juvenile king salmon usually spend one to two years in fresh water before migrating out to sea. They will remain in the ocean from three to five years before returning to the Kenai River in one of two distinct runs. The early run usually begins with a few fish turning up in late April, although it normally doesn't peak until the second week of June. The second group of fish begins arriving at the end of June and often peaks around the third week of July. Many of the second-run fish have spent additional time at sea and tend to be larger.

There's almost universal agreement that early morning is the best time to go king fishing, and most king salmon landed in the Kenai River are caught by backtrolling. Backtrolling, in general, is the same

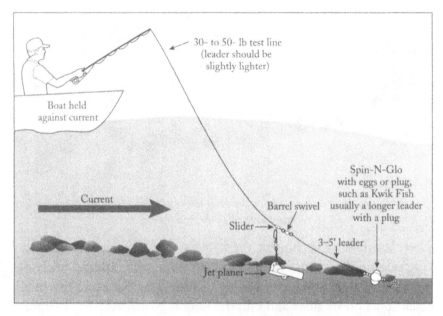

30- to 50- lb test line
(leader should be
slightly lighter)

Boat held
against current

Current

Spin-N-Glo
with eggs or plug,
such as Kwik Fish
usually a longer leader
with a plug

Barrel swivel

Slider

3–5' leader

Jet planer

as pulling any plug above a hole. When fishing kings, however, you want to get deep. To accomplish this most anglers use a jet planer on a slide swivel, followed by a leader of 3 to 5 feet. The favorite plug of many Kenai River anglers is a large Kwikfish (size 14 or 15). When bait is allowed, a small slice of sardine is often attached in order to give it that fishy smell. It's also common to see a flame or chartreuse Spin-N-Glo (basically a plastic ball with flanges that act like a propeller, spinning the lure in the current) often used in conjunction with a large gob of salmon eggs.

A variation of this method is backbouncing, which entails trading the jet planer for a very large round sinker, weighing between 1 and 12 ounces—enough weight to keep in touch with the bottom while periodically lifting and setting (bouncing) the rig in front of the boat.

A rather stout rod is required. Most use a 7- or 8-foot bait-caster with a recommended lure weight of up to 5 ounces, and a good-quality level wind reel.

With either method it's the boat driver or drift boat paddler's job to hold the craft against the current, crisscrossing a particular hole or moving slowly along a riffle or along the bank. This process requires a great deal of concentration, especially on the lower river, where there

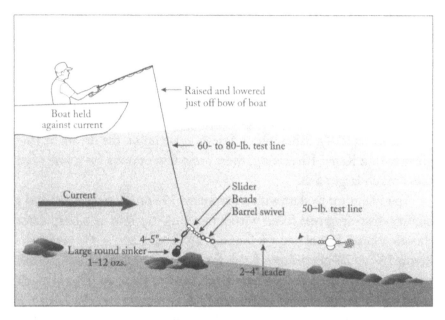

are not only rocks and gravel bars to watch out for but also an incredibly large number of other anglers and boats. If you haven't done this before, especially in a powerboat, it's best to initially explore the river with someone who has, or to spend the money for a guide and see how it is done.

One more technique that is commonly used, especially in the middle river, below Skilak Lake, is the drift method. This is basically the same setup used for rainbows, motoring above a hole and drifting through with a slinky-style sinker. It's the same rig seen in the diagram on page 114. In this case, however, the weight is much larger and the fly is replaced with a Spin-N-Glo and eggs.

While the lower Kenai remains the most popular part of the river to fish for kings, the middle river sees its fair share of action as well. Although the water is faster in the middle river, and there are a larger number of natural obstructions to watch out for, there are also fewer boats around. Those looking for an even more peaceful king-fishing experience may just be in luck. The river below Skilak Lake is closed to guides and is drift-only on Mondays in May, June, and July, offering an excellent respite for rafters and drift boaters looking to land a king.

For fly-fishers, or anyone hoping to catch a king from shore, the

Kenai River can be a tough taskmaster. The river's current and silt-laced waters can make it difficult to even hook a king, let alone chase one of these Titans down the shoreline and land it. The best bet for fly-fishers is to head to one of the streams of the lower peninsula, to the Ninilchik River, Deep Creek, or the Anchor River, which open for several weekends in a row, beginning with Memorial Day weekend. For the intrepid fly-fisher who refuses to give up on the dream of tangling with a Kenai River king, there are a few options for going after these much larger fish.

You will want to start with a minimum 11- or 12-weight rod and a quality disc-drag reel filled with a fast sink-tip line or a deepwater shooting head. Use about a 4-foot tapered leader, and at the very minimum 18- to 20-pound test. Look for likely resting spots, behind obstructions or in deep holes where kings tend to stack up. This is much more easily accomplished by boat, which also gives you the luxury of chasing the fish once it is hooked. Plan on using a large (size 1/0 or 2/0) weighted fly: a Flash Fly, Bunny Leech, or Wiggle Tail. When you do get a strike, be sure to set the hook hard; these fish are notorious for having tough mouths. And whatever you do, avoid the temptation to palm the reel—there's no hope of slowing these fish down, and you could easily break a finger.

Again, because kings tend to run deep, there are simply not many places amenable to fishing from shore. One place that is suitable is the confluence of the Moose River and the Kenai, at the Izaak Walton Recreation Site, in Sterling. You will actually be fishing a small section of the Moose River, below the Sterling Highway Bridge. There is very little current and fish often use this as a holding area to rest on their journey. Try one of these large flies, or any variety of gaudy streamer, to elicit a response. Almost like fishing a lake, you will want to allow time for your fly to sink and then experiment, retrieving it at various speeds. Unfortunately for the king fisher, when the sockeye arrive, this area can get glutted with fishermen, making it difficult to even have much room for a back cast. If it's a late or weak sockeye run, this is the place to try.

Sockeye or Red Salmon

*Dark blue-black back with silvery sides. No distinct spots on back,
dorsal fin, or tail.*

Not only much more numerous than king salmon, sockeye tend to run close to shore, making them the salmon of choice for bank anglers. In fact, the most viable way to catch these fish is from shore, the only advantage of a boat being the ability to find a more secluded piece of property from which to cast.

Red salmon generally spend their first two years of life in fresh water before migrating out to sea, where they will remain for two to three years before they return to spawn. Adults average 4 to 8 pounds and are most easily identified by their dark blue back. Sometimes actually referred to as bluebacks, they are one of the few salmon that have no distinct spots on their back, tail, or fins. These are the salmon often seen in pictures, usually in the later stages of spawning, with crimson bodies and dark green heads—a time of life when they are not worth catching.

There are two runs of sockeye on the Kenai, the first arriving in mid-June. This is a small run, headed for the Russian River. The later, much larger run usually enters the river in early July, peaking near the end of the month. It's not uncommon during this time to see an estimated twenty thousand fish entering the river per day, sparking a fishing frenzy from Cooper Landing to Cook Inlet. Over the past decade sportfishermen have averaged a harvest of approximately one hundred thousand fish per year.

Since sockeye travel only a few feet from shore, it's not necessary

Spawning sockeye salmon adults develop dull green-colored heads and brick-red to scarlet bodies.

to cast very far ahead. Most Kenai River red fishermen employ a technique commonly referred to as the Kenai flip. This technique involves a Coho Fly. Here's where things get confusing. This fly, no more than a few strands of bucktail tied to a long-shank hook, has absolutely nothing to do with coho salmon. And it need not be fished with a fly-rod. Even in waters designated as "fly-fishing only," you may use a spinning outfit as long as your terminal tackle consists of a single-hook unweighted fly. Then, at a minimum of 18 inches above the fly, a sinker large enough to keep in contact with the bottom is attached. With only about 15 feet of line out, this rig is flipped a few feet upstream and allowed to drift, or pulled downstream, slightly ahead of the current, next to shore. When it reaches a position a few feet down-river, it is pitched ahead again, beginning the whole process over. If at any time the sinker stops, the hook should be set and set hard.

Anyone who has witnessed or used this technique knows there is a knack to it. They also know that the fish that are being caught either bite out of frustration or, in most cases, are being "lined"—in other words, snagged in the mouth. As long as they are being hooked in the mouth this technique is perfectly legal, although how sporting it is, is a question we each need to answer for ourselves.

The debate has long raged over whether red salmon actually even bite. There is certainly no doubt that sockeye are the least likely of any salmon to strike. This may be due to the fact that when young red salmon are primarily plankton feeders and therefore are much less likely to feed on the large baitfish that many lures and flies represent.

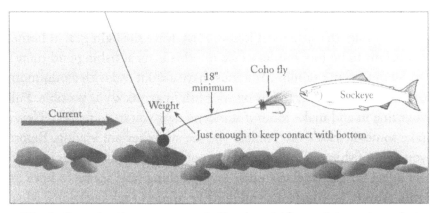

Flip the line a few feet upstream and allow it to drift or pull downstream just ahead of the current, next to the shore.

A growing number of fly-fishers thus maintain that with a small, sparse pattern they are able to elicit a response. Many use a Battle Creek or Polar Shrimp, tied on a size 6 or 8 hook, or they may use a Comet in any combination of orange, yellow, or chartreuse. These flies are fished with a 7- or 8-weight rod, sink-tip line, in a standard down-and-across presentation. The trick is getting the fly to where the fish are, especially in a fast current. Therefore, various fly lines or the addition of a little weight might be necessary. Whatever the technique, fishing for reds with this type of gear is a great deal of fun. These fish are known for their searing runs, and pound for pound their strength may be unparalleled.

Finding enough room to play a fish on light tackle, however, can be difficult at the peak of sockeye season. In most instances red fishing on the Kenai is synonymous with *combat fishing*. This is a term that conjures up all kinds of negative images, but combat fishing is not necessarily bad. There are many people who actually prefer it. In fact, regulars converge every year on places like the Russian River confluence, the Kenai's most famous combat zone. These people enjoy the festive setting, the camaraderie, and all the fish that usually accompany the crowd. It's all a matter of arriving with a good attitude, planning for a party, and enjoying the carnival atmosphere. And if you are shy, it helps to bring a few friends along.

In order to survive and even enjoy combat fishing, there are a few steadfast rules that you must follow. First, leave the light gear at home. It's meant to be fun, but let's face it—this is meat fishing and there's no room to play a salmon. You must have a stout rod with a minimum of 20-pound test line, and bring your fish in as quickly as possible. Pull your line in and make room if someone near you has a fish on. Never take someone else's spot, unless you are sure they are leaving. Before you begin fishing, it's a good idea to observe what is happening and get a feel for the local customs—every fishing hole seems to have its own. Always be courteous and don't be afraid to ask questions. Most people are enjoying the party and are quite willing to give advice.

There are a multitude of red salmon hot spots along the entire length of the Kenai, from its confluence with the Russian River to Centennial Park in Soldotna. These fish are always moving. It may take them several days to reach the middle or upper river. And since they are often entering the stream in fits and starts, it pays to move along with them. If fishing near Soldotna is slow, but was good yesterday, it would be well worth finding a new place upriver—especially if you are lucky enough to be the first to arrive there.

Coho or Silver Salmon

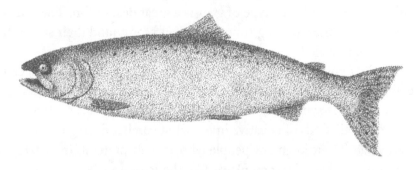

Greenish-blue back with silvery sides. Small black spots on the back, dorsal fin, and usually on the upper lobe of the tail only.

There's simply no mistaking the coho's willingness to strike, and its reputation as an acrobat, making it a favorite among fly-fishers. Averaging 8 to 12 pounds, the coho, also known as the silver salmon, is

Spawning silver salmon adults develop greenish–black heads and dark brown to maroon bodies.

revered for its power and fight as well.

As their name implies, they are silver in color and can be identified by their black gums and the small black spots on their back, dorsal fin, and the upper lobe of their tail. When they are spawning their bodies turn slightly crimson, their heads a greenish-brown.

As juveniles they will typically spend from one to three years in fresh water, with some remaining for as long as five years. They will then venture out to sea for 12 to 18 months before returning to spawn.

The first run of silvers in the Kenai usually begins returning in late July, peaking in mid-August. The second run begins in early September and is present throughout the end of the season, which usually concludes on the last day of September.

In years when there is a strong return, these fish can be found throughout the river. And because of their aggressiveness, anglers use a variety of means to catch them. Backtrolling is popular in the middle and lower sections of the river, using the same technique described for king salmon only with lighter gear and smaller lures. Because silvers tend to hold in deep pockets and even in slack water, casting a spinner or spoon is also an option. A Vibrax is the preferred spinner in the deep holes below Skilak Lake. Cast a Vibrax with a medium- to fast-action rod, and about a 12-pound test line.

For fly-fishers an 8-weight rod is ideal, although some prefer a 9-foot 7-weight. The silvers' propensity for long tireless runs makes a quality disc-drag reel, and adequate backing, critical. In shallow areas a floating line with a 9-foot leader of 8 to 12 pounds is best. When fishing tidal waters or deep slow-moving pockets, a variety of sink-tip lines with a 4-foot leader may be a better choice. If possible align yourself above the fish and cast slightly down-and-across, allowing the fly to swing into the fish's field of view. It's very important to vary your retrieve, especially in slower water.

When silvers are mentioned the first thing that comes to mind is any variety of flash fly. All are effective on coho, however, in shallow, rather clear water, or on bright sunny days, you may have more success with less conspicuous patterns. The purple or black Egg-Sucking Leech or the olive Woolly Bugger, as well as the Bunny Leech, are very productive under these conditions.

If you are feeling adventurous, or if you happen to be lucky enough to see silvers rising, give a dry fly a shot. Coho have been known to occasionally strike or be coaxed into striking the surface—and with their usual carefree abandon. Try a Pink Pollywog, a gaudy concoction tied with spun deer hair, or even a mouse pattern.

Pink or Humpback Salmon

Very large spots on the back and very large oval blotches on both tail lobes.
Very small scales.

Pink salmon, often referred as humpies or humpbacks, are the most maligned members of the salmon family. This is probably due to their small size (about 3 pounds on average) and because they deteriorate fairly quickly on entering fresh water. But don't let this deter you. Taken on light tackle, and near the ocean, pinks are extremely formidable fighters. And despite what anyone says, when caught fresh they are quite good on the grill.

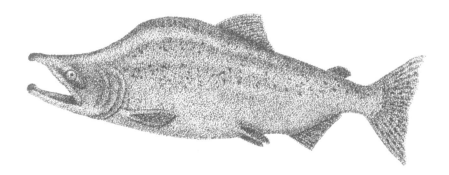

Spawning adults take on a dull gray coloration on the back and upper sides with a creamy white color below. Males develop a pronounced hump.

Pinks are not only distinguished by their size, but by the large oval spots on their tails and back, and by their noticeably smaller scales. Once they enter fresh water pinks immediately begin to turn from silver to green, and the males develop that pronounced hump that gives them their nickname.

They have a distinctive two-year lifecycle, heading to sea as hatchlings and returning to spawn after two years. They begin to show up in fresh water in late July and run through mid-August. In the Kenai River the populations of pinks returning on even numbered years (2004, 2006, 2008) are by far the highest. Because they return in such high numbers and are willing to strike just about any spinner, they are a good choice for young or novice anglers. Use the same techniques you would for silvers, slightly downsizing your equipment. Pinks, for instance, are best taken on light spinning gear or a 4- or 5-weight fly rod. They are not finicky and will readily hit any lure or bright colored fly flashed in front of them. Fish near the ocean, preferably in the intertidal zone. One of the best places is Cunningham Park, located on Beaver Loop Road, in the city of Kenai.

When it comes to pinks, don't let the naysayer's opinions dissuade you. They are fun to catch and provide nonstop action.

Combat fishing at the confluence of the Kenai and Russian Rivers.

CHAPTER 12

Tributaries of the Kenai River

The Russian River

Red Salmon: First run mid-June to mid-July. Second run mid-July to mid-August.
Silver Salmon: Early August through September.
Rainbow Trout and Dolly Varden: Fishing is good from opening day well into September, usually peaking in late July and August, when large numbers of trout are feeding on salmon eggs.

It can be the best of times and the worst of times. For many of us it is a tale of two rivers. On the one hand, the Russian River, a fly-only catch-and-release trout fishery, represents the best opportunity for bank anglers to go after the same native rainbows that inhabit the main-stem Kenai. It is an opportunity to cast for these magnificent creatures in a shallow clearwater stream, often sight fishing, on your own, with no need for a guide. An experience, that between salmon runs, can be surprisingly peaceful.

On the other hand, with the return of the sockeye, a free-for-all ensues. What is considered rude on most rivers—walking through someone's hole or casting in close proximity—is commonplace and even accepted when combat fishing. It's something that must be tolerated, and which, quite frankly, can be difficult if you are trying to drift a dry fly toward a waiting rainbow trout.

One way to resolve this is with an open mind. Be prepared for either scenario. Bring two rods if necessary. Have a 6-weight fly-rod for rainbows; and if it's too crowded, switch to heavier gear and join the melee or simply go elsewhere. As with much of fishing in Alaska, it's all a matter of timing. If you are coming to the Russian for reds and they're not there, or if you want to fish rainbows and simply find it too crowded for your taste, come back. Things can change here rather quickly, sometimes even in a matter of hours.

Lower Russian River

Scenery: 4.5
Wilderness experience: 1
Tip: Don't be discouraged by large numbers of people. Either come back later or join the fray. The fishing here is great.

The majority of fishermen begin their day at the Forest Service campground, located at Milepost 52 of the Sterling Highway. The run timing for red salmon on the Russian River is about the same as the main-stem Kenai, usually peaking in mid-June and again in late July. Most anglers use the same techniques and rules for combat fishing described in chapter 11 on red salmon. Although in much smaller numbers, silvers also spawn in the Russian River, providing a somewhat less crowded alternative from August through September.

The angler does need to be aware of special regulations on the Russian River. This is a "fly-fishing only" area, which means that a spinning rod can still be used, but only with an unweighted single-hook artificial fly, with the gap between the point and shank of the hook no more than ⅜ inch.

For trout anglers this small clear stream is a true gem. Large num-

The Kenai Lakes trail, on the way to the Upper Russian River

bers of native 'bows remain after spawning or follow the sockeye here to feast on their decaying flesh or the flood of eggs they leave behind. Early in the season, if the reds have yet to show, try dead drifting a nymph pattern. You might also try casting a Muddler Minnow or sculpin pattern to these trout, which are easily spotted on the edge of riffles or near overhanging banks. With the massive influx of red salmon, go to an egg pattern or flesh fly. Sometimes you can actually see rainbow trout lined up, waiting for scraps below the cleaning tables. Those of a more traditional ilk, or those who simply want a change of pace, should not be bashful about breaking out the dry flies. While they're certainly nowhere near as productive as an egg pattern, it is possible at any time of year in this clear water to convince a trout to rise. Try an Adams or Adams Parachute, Black Gnat, or Blue Winged Olive in size 14 to 18. There's nothing quite like the thrill of coaxing one of these beauties to the surface.

Fishing the "other" Russian River, above Lower Russian Lake

Upper Russian River

Scenery: 5
Wilderness Experience: 4.5
Tip: Best fishing for rainbows and Dollies is at either end of the river, near the lakes, in July and early August when red salmon are spawning. Keep an eye out for bears.

Another option for the more adventurous fly-fisher is to head to the "other" Russian River. The one farther upstream, running for about 8 miles between the Upper and Lower Russian Lakes, the one off-limits to salmon fishing. Here the trout aficionado will find the current much slower than in the lower river, meandering in large deep pockets, the banks unblemished by the hordes of visitors flooding its lower reaches. This is an area where you rarely encounter other fishermen and where bears still outnumber people. It does, however, require a little extra effort to reach this part of the river. Be prepared for a hike or mountain bike up the Russian Lakes Trail, described in detail in chapter 6.

Sockeye salmon, late in the season on the Russian, dropping eggs for hungry rainbows and Dollies.

The best fishing on this part of the river generally tends to be near its inlet at the lower lake, about 4 miles in, or at its outlet at the upper lake, a 12-mile trip from the Russian River Campground. The fishing will heat up throughout the river as the reds return, drawing large numbers of rainbows as well as Dolly Varden out of the lakes. The fish do tend to be somewhat smaller than those inhabiting the lower river. The fish in this section usually run 12 to 18 inches, although there are a few that regularly breach the 20-inch mark.

Along with Forest Service cabins at either lake, there is also the Aspen Flats Cabin, located on the river at Mile 9 of the trail. The best sites to pitch a tent are found on the lakes. With camping along the river limited, and bear activity high, you need some backcountry experience if you're going to venture into this area.

Anyone visiting the Russian River might want to take a break from fishing and check out the Russian River Falls. This is an opportunity to witness one of the most dramatic spectacles of nature—thousands of red and silver salmon fighting their way to their ancestral grounds, leaping with near-impossible acrobatics, mind-boggling power, and an irrepressible will. Located below Lower Russian Lake, it is an easy 2.5-mile walk to the viewing platforms and a sight you will not soon forget.

Quartz Creek and Ptarmigan Creek

Note: Salmon are spawning by the time they reach these streams; fishing for them is not allowed.
Scenery: 4.5
Wilderness Experience: 2.5
Tip: Fishing for rainbow trout and Dolly Varden is best in July and August. Cast an egg pattern behind the spawning salmon.

Technically these two small streams are not tributaries of the Kenai River. They are, however, an integral part of the same watershed. Quartz and Ptarmigan provide important spawning grounds and at various times of the year host many of the same fish that normally occupy the Kenai River. While a handful of these large rainbows and Dolly Varden do take up summer residence in these streams, fishing for them can be slow until the return of the salmon in late July. By the time the sockeye reach these streams, they have turned bright crimson and are not worth catching, but they are sure to be followed by legions of hungry Dolly Varden, voraciously vacuuming up their favorite food—eggs. And many of these fish, especially in Quartz Creek, are as large as salmon, some in excess of 25 inches.

Ptarmigan Creek is easily accessed from a campground at Milepost 23 of the Seward Highway. And Quartz Creek can be reached anywhere from Milepost 41 to Milepost 44 of the Sterling Highway, where the stream parallels the roadway. It can also be reached from Quartz Creek Road, which turns off the highway at Milepost 45.

Before the salmon show up, it's best on either stream to move around a lot. Work various holes with a nymph or dry fly, keeping an eye out for fish or trying to spot a rise. While fishing this time of year can be slow, it does offer a rather tranquil alternative to combat fishing. And even when the salmon do return, it remains a somewhat peaceful

A nice Dolly Varden on Quartz Creek

affair because there are usually only trout fishermen on these streams.

Anytime the salmon are present, from the end of July through August, fish behind them, dead drifting an egg pattern. Be sure to change colors and adjust the amount of weight you are using. Then, hang on—this is Alaskan fishing at its best.

CHAPTER 13

Streams of the Southern Kenai Peninsula

The Kasilof River

King Salmon: First run mid-May to late June. Second run early July to season's end, usually July 31.
Red Salmon: Late June to early August.
Silver Salmon: Late July to mid-September.
Steelhead (Crooked Creek): August through November.
Scenery: 3.5
Wilderness Experience: 1.5
Tip: In most cases, because of the extremely low visibility of the water, use bait. Or use a very flashy spinner, spoon, or fly.

When it comes to salmon fishing, this stream is often considered the Kenai River alternative. Flowing out of Tustumena Lake and crossing the Sterling Highway at Mile 109.5, the Kasilof supports two runs of king salmon that usually begin arriving in mid-May and run through

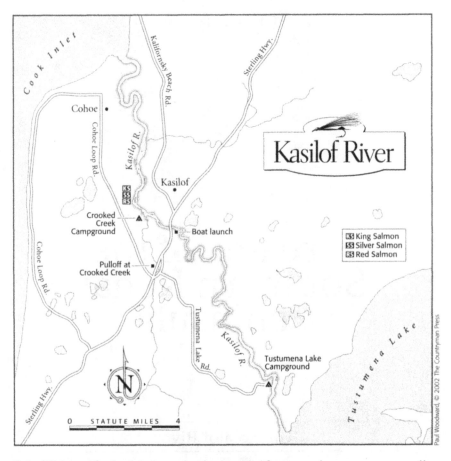

July. This swift glacial river also has a significant sockeye return, usually beginning in June and peaking by mid-July.

Shore anglers for both species flock to Crooked Creek Campground, located about 2 miles down Cohoe Loop Road, which intersects the Sterling Highway at Milepost 111. Though quite a bit of shoreline is open for angling, this state-run campground can become very crowded at the height of the season. When these conditions exist, it is wise to use heavy gear and employ the same rules for combat fishing as you would on the Kenai or Russian Rivers. The techniques for catching these fish are also the same, with most anglers employing the Kenai flip.

Backtrolling for king salmon, and later for silvers, is also popular. The only change in gear from the Kenai River is a shorter leader (24 to 36 inches) because of the shallow stream conditions. The Division of

State Parks maintains a wayside and launch site for drift boats, located where the river and highway meet, at Milepost 109.5 of the Sterling Highway. If fishing has been slow on the Kenai River, expect large numbers of displaced salmon fishermen to descend on this small stream, glutting it with drift boats. On the other hand, if the Kenai is seeing strong returns of salmon, a float down the Kasilof is likely to be the more relaxing of the two. The king salmon on the Kasilof, however, are a partially enhanced run and are not nearly as large as those on the Kenai. In fact, only a few each year exceed 40 pounds.

The silvers that return to the Kasilof are generally an early run, arriving in July and tapering off in early September. Because of the extremely low visibility of the water, many anglers opt for a cluster of salmon eggs. If not using bait, a very flashy spinner, spoon, or fly is required to get the attention of these fish. One option is to fish Crooked Creek, which opens in August. It enters the Kasilof at the campground that bears its name. The creek can also be accessed at a small pullout on the Sterling Highway, just before Cohoe Loop Road. Crooked Creek also holds a small return of steelhead, which begin to show up in August. Many overwinter and can be caught in the Kasilof in April and May (Crooked Creek is closed at this time).

Its glacial, silty water makes the Kasilof a poor choice for the traditional fly-fisher. Those looking to fish trout or Dolly Varden would be much better off heading north to the upper Kenai or south to the Anchor River.

The Anchor River, Deep Creek, and the Ninilchik River

King Salmon: Late May to mid-June.
Silver Salmon: July to mid-September.
Dolly Varden: July through October.
Steelhead: Mid-August until ice-up, usually sometime in November.
Scenery: 3.5
Wilderness Experience: 2.5
Tip: With the only steelhead fishing on the Kenai Peninsula, these streams offer a great way to extend the season.

Kings on the Ninilchik River

Beneath an impressive backdrop of dormant snowcapped volcanoes, the Sterling Highway snakes its way along the icy waters of Cook Inlet, passing a trio of tempting streams. All three support strong runs of silver salmon, sea-run Dolly Varden, and autumn steelhead. They also represent the best opportunity for shore anglers to tangle with a king salmon. The king fishery is a weekend-only event, running from Saturday through Monday, beginning on Memorial Day weekend. As you can imagine these streambanks get crowded, making it wise to fish at off hours. Try early in the morning. And if the salmon continue to filter in throughout the weekend, Sunday night can also be a good time to go.

While spinning gear is common, most anglers prefer a 10-weight fly-rod. Some use traditional streamers, Bunny Leeches, or Flash Flies, even gigantic egg patterns. With only a short window of opportunity, however, most forsake tradition and go with the real thing—fresh salmon eggs—even on a fly-rod. They simply let a gob of eggs on a size 4/0-hook bounce through a likely looking run. Many people

Silver fishing near the mouth of the Anchor River

also employ the use of a small Spin-N-Glo, along with eggs and a sinker about 18 inches above the bait.

The king salmon in these streams reach the 15- to 25-pound range, rarely surpassing 40 pounds. And only on the Ninilchik River, because this run is enhanced, are you allowed to keep fishing after you have retained a king. On all other streams, including the Kenai River, you must stop fishing once you have kept a king.

Silver salmon return from late July through mid-September. The best fishing is definitely early in the morning, under low-light conditions. Bait is usually allowed until September first, but be sure to check the regulations. Otherwise, employ the same methods described in chapter 11 on silver salmon.

During and between runs there is the added bonus of Dolly Varden. Present from July through October, these large sea-run fish provide excellent sport and an opportunity, especially on the Anchor River, to unsheath the 4-weight fly-rod and break out the dry flies. They will also readily take flesh flies and any egg pattern.

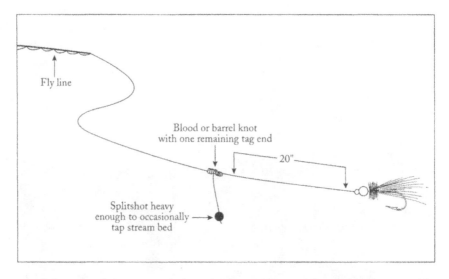

Fly line

Blood or barrel knot
with one remaining tag end

20"

Splitshot heavy
enough to occasionally
tap stream bed

Most fly-fishers agree that the best time on these streams is mid- to late September, during the peak of the steelhead run. Steelhead first become available in August, although this fishery continues until freeze-up, which on mild years can come as late as Thanksgiving. These small runs of fish are the northernmost extreme of Alaska's steelhead and are strictly catch-and-release. Therefore, they should always be handled with care and promptly unhooked.

Steelhead in these waters usually stay in the 8- to 12-pound class, making a 7- or 8-weight fly-rod sufficient. Being shallow and narrow streams, especially by steelhead standards, a basic floating line works best. One very successful method is to use a 9- or 10-foot leader, cutting only one tag end on the knot between the leader and tippet, as if fishing a dropper. On the remaining tag-end, experiment with split-shot until you are occasionally tapping the streambed, leaving about 20 inches of tippet between weight and fly. Favorite flies are the Battle Creek, Polar Shrimp, purple or black Egg-Sucking Leech, or a sparkling purple Woolly Bugger. Any variety of egg pattern can also be very effective. This rig can be difficult to cast, but it works well on any narrow fast-moving stream, not only with steelhead, but with trout and silver salmon as well.

You can easily access the Ninilchik River from one of two campgrounds run by Alaska State Parks, at Mile 134.5 and Mile 135.5 of the

Steelhead

Sterling Highway. Deep Creek can be reached from a state recreation site at Mile 137.3. Though these two streams are close to each other, their water sources are not the same. It's entirely possible for one to have high turbid water, and the other to be completely fishable. So always check out both streams.

The Anchor River is another 20 miles farther south, near the village of Anchor Point. Most anglers turn off the Sterling Highway at Milepost 157, near the Anchor River Inn, and follow the signs to the Anchor River State Recreation Area. There are five major camping areas and pullouts along this road, which eventually terminates near the beach. Many steelhead and Dolly fishermen prefer fishing farther upstream and will continue down the highway, past Anchor Point, to the North Fork Road, which turns off the Sterling Highway at Mile 164.3.

CHAPTER 14

The Quiet Alternative

After we shook hands, it was obvious—we were looking each other over, checking each other out, asking ourselves: Do I really want to spend two days in a canoe with this guy?

It all started when my friend Charlie bowed out of our trip at the last minute. He suggested as an alternative that Frank, a colleague of his at the U.S. Fish and Wildlife Service, take his place.

He must have sensed my hesitation. "He's a good guy," he tried to convince me. "You two will get along just fine."

I must admit: an internal warning beacon had come on, dredging up various situations of the past. Those rare but uncomfortable occasions stuck in close quarters with an obstinate coworker or, even worse, having to endure an overbearing fishing partner. But I really wanted to go. This was one of the few places on the Kenai Peninsula I had yet to explore, and the promise of silver salmon stacked up like cordwood kept pestering me.

Okay, I agreed rather reluctantly. And now here we were, two strangers about to set out for the backcountry, quietly sizing each other up. The only consolation: It was a two-hour drive shuttling vehicles from Captain Cook State Park on Cook Inlet to our launch site on the

Paddling the Swanson River in search of salmon

Swanson River in Sterling. We would have plenty of time to get to know each other, and if it looked as though we were completely incompatible, there was still a small window of opportunity to abandon our plans.

It wasn't long after Frank settled into the passenger seat that I sensed things would work out. We shared an almost overriding appreciation for all things outdoors and were both excited to be heading somewhere new. In fact, by the time we reached the launch site, our only worry was the weather. We had been experiencing a slow insidious rain all day, but now, as we pulled up to the small staging area, we found ourselves in the middle of a giant cloudburst. Large stinging raindrops were pelting the ground all around us, erupting in tiny explosions of mud and sounding a drumbeat of implied warning on the belly of the overturned canoe.

But things would be all right. It wasn't like this area was completely new to me. I'd once spent a long day paddling from Gene Lake down to this spot, and many times I'd worked my way upstream to dab dry flies for trout. Still, I had no idea how long it would take us to reach the coast from here. And with only one full day for our journey, and the afternoon fading fast, we decided to head out, agreeing that we would go no more than three hours before making camp.

We spent that time paddling through an immense bank of fog interspersed with sheets of rain. But our conversation—about other trips we'd taken or large fish we'd caught—flowed as slow and easy as the current, turning what otherwise might have been torture into a mere nuisance.

Then, just as the light was waning, there it appeared—the perfect campsite, on a knoll overlooking a sharp bend in the river. And as we began to unload the canoe, we realized something. Miraculously, the rain had stopped. We shared a couple of beers by the fire and marveled at the canopy of sky opening above us, the stars beginning to wink between softly swaying boughs of Sitka spruce, all of it awash in the pale blue light of a full moon.

We set out early the next morning. The air was still. The sun was rising just above the mountains, penetrating the few remaining traces

FRANK HARRIS

A Swanson River silver

of charcoal-colored clouds—an omen for the day to come.

We rigged our rods and paddled hard, keeping an eye out for the telltale signs of swirling silver, pointing out the recently planted moose tracks along the river bottom or the muskrat families scurrying along the shoreline.

"There they are" came Frank's sudden announcement from the bow of the boat. And there was nothing telltale about it. This was an army en masse, literally clogging the long deep hole, kicking up an enormous wake as they circled upstream and down.

Seeing these scores of bright fish, it was nearly impossible to quell the sudden haste and impatience that seized me. I simultaneously climbed ashore and began casting a Wog, a crazy pink monstrosity tied with spun deer hair and designed to fish on the surface. My first cast, however, was met with disdain. It immediately started the water boiling, sending fish by the dozens scattering in all directions. I could tell this would take a little finesse and some stealth.

Moving a little farther downstream in an absurd attempt to fool the same fish, I laid the Wog out again. They didn't scatter, so I cast once more. On this pass a fish emerged from the restless mob. I watched from above, the whole thing playing out in front of me like a slow-motion scene from an action thriller. The silver turned, taking an interest, and following my fly across the entire surface of the stream— only to veer off at the last minute. A scene both stirring and disheartening played before me a second time and even a third.

I knew there was something they liked and didn't like, so I switched to a pink Bunny Leech. No deer hair, but the same color, for all practical purposes the subsurface version of the same fly. Again one emerged from the crowd, this time taking a decisive interest, following only a short distance and striking hard. The fight, all twenty minutes of it, was on—complete with several long runs and a full aerial display of somersaults and cartwheels. A performance that stirred the other residents of the hole into a frenzy.

Neither of us had brought a watch. And I don't know how long we lingered there, long enough to hook a couple more fish. But not knowing how long it would take us to paddle the entire length of the river, we reluctantly decided to move on. Unfortunately, the farther we moved downriver the higher the sun climbed, and the more cautious the fish became. Next time we vowed to leave earlier, so we could make camp at the first sign of silvers. Then we could hit them in the evening and again in the morning, at low light. We would also bring some lighter gear and fish around the salmon for the small trout that thrive in this stream.

Until this point we had not seen another party, but the closer we came to the takeout, the more signs of civilization we saw and the more fishermen we encountered. Still, it was an utterly peaceful trip. We saw moose, plenty of ducks, and, of course, an onslaught of chrome-bright silvers. Above all, I was glad I had taken a chance. I was able to catch a few fish, see a new section of river, and most important, find a new fishing buddy.

The Swanson River

Red Salmon: Very small number in early July.
Silver Salmon: Late July to mid-September.
Rainbow Trout: Small in size but large in number,
throughout the season.
Scenery: 3
Wilderness Experience: 3.5
Tip: Plan a trip down the Swanson before moose season, which
usually opens September 1.

The Swanson River can be easily accessed from a landing at the end of Swanson River Road, which turns off the Sterling Highway at Mile 83.5. This is the middle section of the river. From here, with the mild current, you can actually paddle upstream and dab dry flies for rainbow trout, or head the 24 miles downstream to Cook Inlet (a two-day trip if you are planning to spend any time at all fishing).

The river originates from Gene Lake, in the heart of the Swan Lake/Swanson River Canoe System. It requires a full day of paddling and portaging to reach Gene Lake; from there it is an often-arduous 19-mile trek to the landing on Swanson River Road. For more information, please turn to chapter 6, on the Swan Lake/Swanson River Canoe System (the Swanson River Route).

The journey downstream, while less difficult, is not one you want to make with a new canoe. The water is shallow, and with many exposed—and barely exposed—gravel bars and rocks, you are sure to put plenty of scrapes and scratches on the bottom of your boat. There are numerous campsites, but many require crossing marshy terrain. Your best bet for finding the least crowded silver fishing is 6 to 10 miles downstream, although cohos in this shallow clear water are known to be finicky.

Until the silvers begin to show up in August, plan on fishing rainbow trout in the 10- to 15-inch range. These fish are easy to spot and will readily rise for a variety of dry flies. In the deeper holes and along cut-banks try a streamer or leech, or cast a small spinner. For silvers try a Bunny Leech or Flash Fly, preferably in the early morning or evening.

You can access the lower reaches of the river from the canoe landing at Captain Cook State Recreation Area, at the end of North Kenai Road. This is a good place to spend the day fishing for silvers, although it can get crowded.

While you are likely to encounter other fishermen or canoeists at any time along this river, most of the year it remains a very peaceful alternative. During moose season, however, which normally runs for 20 days beginning September first, it becomes a major thoroughfare. This is a time when fishermen looking to "get away from it all" might be better off going elsewhere. If you plan on moose hunting, though, be sure to bring your rod. There's no sense missing out on a good thing.

Resurrection Creek

Pink Salmon: July to mid-August.
Scenery: 4.5
Wilderness Experience: 2

Think pink. I can't say enough about this often-maligned member of the salmon family. This little brother is a worthy opponent when caught early and with the right equipment. On a 5-weight fly-rod, or a midweight spinning outfit, the pink quickly becomes an equal to any of its larger cousins.

Pinks begin their annual return in July, and one of the best places to find them is at the headwaters of Resurrection Creek, in the tiny village of Hope. This small community, just south of Anchorage, is a true taste of old-time Alaska. It's worth the drive simply to experience the rough-and-ready charm of a town so steeped in history, where the discovery of gold predates the Klondike and where mining still takes place today.

Located off the Sterling Highway (at Milepost 57), down a section of road known appropriately as the Hope Cutoff, Resurrection Creek is also a place where there is relatively little angling pressure. It is a place where the pink salmon return in large numbers, fresh from the ocean and actively feeding. The best fishing is in town, along the first few miles of the creek. The current can be fast in places, though there are plenty of pools where large numbers of fish hold. Pinks are susceptible to any flashy spinner or spoon, or to Flash Flies or bright streamers, such as a Black-Nosed Dace or Blue Smolt. Try a Polar Shrimp or any gaudy egg pattern, such as the Two-Egg Sperm Fly.

Those looking for other "quiet alternatives," should consider some of the tributaries of the Kenai River. Ptarmigan Creek, the upper Russian River, and Quartz Creek could all have been included in this category. They are excellent options, especially for fly- fishers who want to make a break from the crowd.

PART IV

SALT WATER

CHAPTER 15

Resurrection Bay (Seward)

Resurrection Bay

King Salmon (Lowell Creek and the small boat harbor): Early June
to mid-August.
Silver Salmon: July to mid-September.
Pink Salmon: Late June to mid-August.
Dolly Varden: Late April through May.
Halibut: April to late September.
Scenery: 5
Wilderness Experience: 1–3.5

It was here, in a campground outside Seward, that my Alaskan adventure truly began. I had been driving for nearly 10 days, the money about gone, and my mother's warnings still ringing in my ears. With the rain showing no signs of letting up and a thick curtain of fog hanging over the town, I was beginning to wonder what I had gotten myself into.

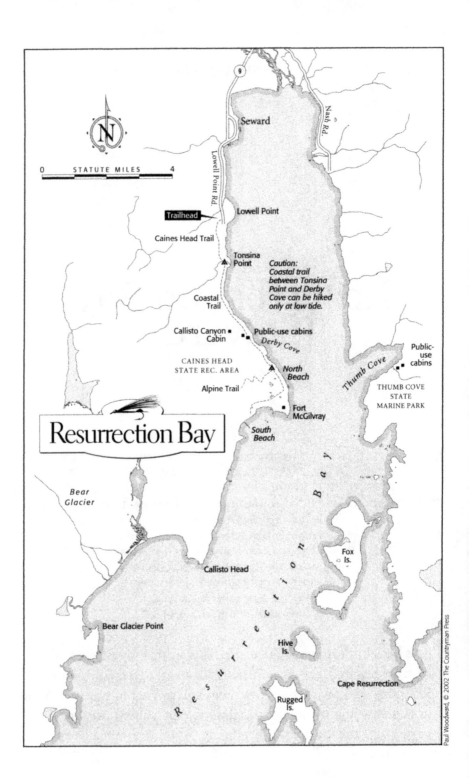

N

0 STATUTE MILES 4

9

Seward

Nash Rd.

Lowell Point Rd.

Trailhead

Lowell Point

Caines Head Trail

Tonsina
Point

*Caution:
Coastal trail
between Tonsina
Point and Derby
Cove can be hiked
only at low tide.*

Coastal
Trail

Callisto Canyon
Cabin

Public-use cabins

Derby Cove

CAINES HEAD
STATE REC. AREA

North
Beach

Thumb Cove

Public-
use
cabins

THUMB COVE
STATE
MARINE PARK

Alpine Trail

Fort
McGilvray

Resurrection Bay

South
Beach

*Bear
Glacier*

Resurrection Bay

Callisto Head

Fox
Is.

Bear Glacier Point

Hive
Is.

Cape Resurrection

Rugged
Is.

Paul Woodward, © 2002 The Countryman Press

For three straight days I wandered on the edge of Resurrection Bay, something I could only sense was very large. I could smell it on the breeze, taste it in that heavy, oyster-shell air that follows low tide. But was this all there was? I wondered. A drab canvas of brown and gray, shrouded in a perpetual mist.

Then, on the fourth day, I awoke to an unfamiliar brightness, to a tent damp not with rain but with condensation. Dressing quickly I emerged from my nylon hovel as if from a long hibernation, making my way to the edge of the campground and into a changed world. A fresh portrait of Alaska.

To think that for three days I had walked blindly along the verge of this tenuous border, completely oblivious to a world of such magnitude, eclipsed behind nothing but a thin mantle of low-lying clouds.

Now I looked down in wonder on a village that appeared as though it were in peril of being swallowed by the sea, a tiny village tucked among mountains so spectacular it was as if they rose out of some unimaginable dream. Primordial, windswept mountains—white-faced, blue veined, and cloud rimmed. It was unbelievable. All I could do was stand there and take the majesty of it in, feeling dwarfed by its immensity yet lucky to be a part of it.

That was fifteen years ago. Although Seward has grown quite a bit, whenever I return to fish its waters I find myself once again caught by the enormity, the almost indescribable sense of spirit, that is found amidst such raw and overwhelming beauty.

Along with its rugged, natural charm, Resurrection Bay includes some excellent fishing. It is world renowned for the annual Seward Silver Salmon Derby, which runs for nine days, beginning in mid-August. With prize money totaling over $100,000, and $10,000 offered for the largest silver, this event attracts a lot of interest. Fortunately, the run usually peaks in August, just after the derby, and continues strong well into September. And because of the size and grandeur of Resurrection Bay, it rarely feels crowded, particularly with the personal space and freedom provided by a boat.

Skiff rentals are available in Seward. One of the best deals can be found 2 miles south of town, down a winding, pothole-laden road, on a stretch of land called Lowell Point. Here sits Miller's Landing. Situated on the old family homestead, this campground and fish camp truly captures the uniqueness and funky appeal of the "real" Alaska. Of the many services they provide, perhaps the best bargain is their boat rental—a flotilla of skiffs, fitted with 25-horsepower outboards. These boats afford bargain hunters (those with some previous boating experience) the opportunity to ply these rich and very productive waters on their own. For those with less money and a more adventurous spirit, there are also a number of outfitters that rent kayaks. Paddling one of these small boats maintains just about the perfect speed for trolling, and attempting to land a fiery coho from one of them certainly adds to the challenge.

Trolling is the most common method of salmon fishing from any type of boat. Most charter boats and large private vessels are equipped with downriggers, a definite advantage early in the season when the salmon are running deep. Later in the year, when the runs hit in earnest, those in small boats have just as much chance of landing large numbers of fish. The basic setup for trolling includes a trolling or "banana" sinker, and a salmon leader, preferably with a sliding top hook (sold in various sizes at all local tackle shops). Herring, either cut or whole, are attached to the hooks and trailed behind the boat. Bait herring, in various sizes, can also be purchased frozen at just about any tackle shop, supermarket, or department store on the Kenai Peninsula. Before starting out it should be allowed to thaw. Many anglers place a flasher or dodger between the weight and the herring. Those of us who like to keep it simple find this unnecessary. When the salmon are in thick, the scent, along with the flash of the spinning herring, is enough to attract plenty of action. It's important when you first begin trolling to outfit each rod with a different size weight in order to determine at what depth the fish are cruising. If one rod is particularly hot, switch to that size sinker.

The latest advance in trolling is the Rotary Salmon Killer, a plastic harness that attaches to the herring and spins it. It trails a hook, so you simply tie your own leader between this gadget and the sinker.

Another popular method of salmon fishing is "mooching," which

A Resurrection Bay silver salmon

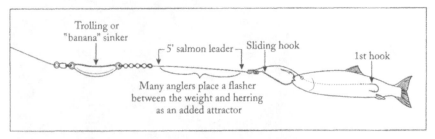

Trolling or
"banana" sinker

5' salmon leader   Sliding hook

1st hook

Many anglers place a flasher
between the weight and herring
as an added attractor

The first hook on the salmon leader goes completely through the eyes. It then goes in and partially out on the same side of the herring, so that just the bend and the tip of the hook are protruding behind the dorsal fin, at about the herring's lateral line. The second hook is then placed through the lips of the bait. Test the rig in the water, next to the boat, and see that the herring is slowly spinning. If so, let out your line (start with 30 or 40 feet) and begin trolling. Let out more line as you go, experiment with different weight sinkers, and keep an eye out for "jumpers," salmon breaking the surface.

employs the same basic setup as the trolling rig. In this case it's common to slide a "hoochy," or rubber squid body, onto the leader over the herring, which is usually cut in half. The bait is simply allowed to drift. The boat operator occasionally puts the motor into gear or the fisherman lifts the rod tip in order to give the rig some action. Some anglers use a hoochy on their trolling rigs as well; the rubber tentacles supply an added bit of enticement.

As the silver salmon begin to move in closer to town in mid- to late August, they can also be readily caught from shore. Locals use a large silver Vibrax spinner or the Pixie spoon. Cast either of these lures along any of the beaches in town, or on Fourth of July Beach, on the east side of the bay. Or try simply dangling cut herring, or fresh salmon eggs, a few feet beneath a large bobber to catch silvers. One of the best places to soak bait is along Lowell Point Road. This narrow road is subject to small rockslides, so it's best to find a decent pullout in which to park and to walk to your fishing spot.

While silvers are the major draw in Seward (it's estimated that about fifty thousand are caught annually), there's much more to Resurrection Bay. It begins in April, when sea-run Dolly Varden hit area beaches. Fish up to 25 inches can be caught on light tackle or fly gear. Any spinner, such as a Rooster Tail or Vibrax, will work well. Fly-rodders will want to fish with a sink-tip line and any streamer. Try a Mickey Fin or a small Lefty's Deceiver. For those who want to get a little way out of town, fish along the beach at Lowell Point. For those who want to get way out of town, take a hike down the coast to Tonsina Point, via the Caines Head Trail. It takes less than an hour to reach the beach at Tonsina Point, the halfway-mark of this trail, which begins at the Lowell Point State Recreation Site. These Dollies tend to run in schools, and fishing for them can be hit or miss—either a lot of action or none at all.

King salmon have been planted in the bay and begin to show up in early June. They run from 15 to 35 pounds and are most easily caught near where they were originally planted as fingerlings—at Lowell Creek or outside the lagoon, south of the small boat harbor. Their feeding habits are similar to silvers. A Vibrax spinner is the favorite lure among king fishermen. The often-crowded conditions on shore, and the casting distance required to reach these fish, can make it difficult on fly-fishers. There are, however, large candlefish and herring patterns tied just for this purpose. Use them, as well as any large streamer or Deceiver, for both kings and silvers.

Kings are also caught by trolling, and it's becoming increasingly popular to troll for winter kings. These so-called feeder kings are probably not destined for Resurrection Bay but are simply migrating through the area. It definitely takes a strong constitution to go out after these fish during winter. It also helps if you have a boat with a cabin.

Halibut fishing out of Seward is extremely popular. Many charter boats venture as far as 50 miles outside of Resurrection Bay for these flatfish, coveted for their white, flaky meat. Halibut average 40 to 80 pounds, but it's not uncommon to return with fish that tip the scales at 200, even 300, pounds. Every year halibut migrate into the bay and are caught by fishermen soaking bait. Those who truly want to experience halibut fishing (and who want to bring an ample supply of meat home with them) should book a charter, especially considering the size of these fish and the distance required to find them.

Many local boat owners fish the nearby capes using a jig or soaking bait for rockfish. Black sea bass and red snapper are a delicacy, and there is always the chance of picking up a lingcod or halibut, especially in the outer reaches, around Rugged Island or Cape Resurrection. Even these areas require a large vessel and skills as a seaman. If you are in a smaller boat, try near Caines Head or the point around Thumb Cove. Be sure to check the regulations, because the open season on many fish, such as the lingcod, has been shortened due to dwindling stocks.

Some of the most fun a fly-fisher can have is going after rockfish. If fishing the deep water off a point or a cape, one member of the party must offer to jig without a hook. This person's task is to coax the fish toward the surface. If fish are congregated in a certain area, this job is not difficult. They will swarm the jig and follow it up. The fly-casters just stand by, armed with a 7- or 8-weight rod, sink-tip or full sinking line, and a weighted, saltwater fly. Among the many options when it comes to flies, try a Lefty's Deceiver, a white tarpon fly, a Comet, even a big Zonker, in sizes 2/0 to 3. In this case, finding the fish is more important than which fly to use. Swarming rockfish will hit just about anything that looks like a baitfish. Some of these fish reach the 6- to 8-pound range and run like crazy. It's important to have a good saltwater line and adequate backing. Certain rockfish, such as the black bass, will also hold around kelp beds, like those found near the Eldorado Narrows, south of Cape Resurrection. Often this means shallower water and a lighter line.

Finding a Place to Stay

Options for lodging in Seward abound, and run the gambit from rustic to formal. They include numerous hotels, motels, and bed & breakfasts. There are several commercially run campgrounds and RV parks, and the city of Seward maintains many beachfront camping areas. These areas can become extremely crowded at the peak of the season, forcing RVs and car campers to move inland.

More remote camping can be found on Tonsina Point, or farther down the trail at Caines Head State Recreation Area. Both spots have picnic shelters, rustic campsites, and basic latrines. The hike from Tonsina Point to Caines Head can only be made at low tide, and requires a 12-hour stay between tides. There are two public-use cabins along the way: the Derby Cove and the Callisto Canyon Cabins. Reservations, made through Alaska State Parks, are required. In fact, anyone planning to make the trip beyond Tonsina Point should check with State Parks first. Not only can the parks department supply you with particulars about the trail, but they also have a great deal of information on this historic area, including Fort McGilvray—a World War II command center, the remains of which still stand at Caines Head.

State Parks also maintains two cabins in Thumb Cove, on the east side of Resurrection Bay. These cabins can only be reached by boat, and because they are extremely popular, reservations must be made well in advance. Like the other cabins, they are fairly rustic but very comfortable.

For adventurers looking to get away from it all, Kenai Fjords National Park has three cabins on the outer coast, between Seward and Homer. They can be difficult to reach, and are usually accessed by air. The best cabin for fishing is the Aialik Bay Cabin, near Pedersen Lagoon, which has large returns of red and silver salmon. The other two cabins have limited fishing opportunities.

CHAPTER 16

Kachemak Bay and Cook Inlet (Homer to Ninilchik)

Kachemak Bay

King Salmon (Homer Spit, Halibut Cove, Seldovia Bay): Mid-May to
early July.
Red Salmon (China Poot Bay): July to mid-August.
Silver Salmon: Late July to mid-September.
Pink Salmon (Tutka Bay and streams on northern shore): Late
June to mid-August.
Dolly Varden: Late April through May.
Halibut: March to late September.
Scenery: 5
Wilderness Experience: 1–5

Whenever I arrive in Homer I'm overcome by that same sense of
wonder that I felt 15 years ago, in Seward, the day the fog finally lifted
and revealed that spectacular landscape. I'm engulfed by that same

feeling each time I round the final bend of the Sterling Highway and find myself confronted by the looming cliffs and jagged spires of Kachemak Bay, and by the vast expanse of open ocean where Cook Inlet and the Gulf of Alaska meet.

Both towns are known for their stunning beauty and excellent fishing—fishing of all kinds. But if Seward's claim to fame is its silver salmon, Homer's is its halibut. In fact, a sign as you enter town touts Homer as the halibut capital of the world. And it's probably right. Every day, throughout the summer, boats return to the harbor with thousands of pounds of this highly sought-after denizen of the deep. It's one of the best-tasting and most versatile fish you can find for the frying pan, grill, or oven.

Fishing for halibut usually begins in March. Fish are available throughout the bay, but they do move around depending on the time of year and the availability of food. Halibut generally tend to move in a little closer to shore early in the season, in May, and are occasionally even caught off the end of the Homer Spit. The Spit, a natural jetty that penetrates several miles into the bay, is a major component of Homer's geography, the center of any activity pertaining to the sea. The boat harbor is located there, a theater as well as a series of small shops and boardwalks, and a few landmarks like the Salty Dog Saloon. It's from here that most boats head to the halibut grounds, north toward Bluff Point, or across the bay, outside of the village of Seldovia. As the season progresses, the majority of boats head farther out into Cook Inlet. This is open water, where conditions can change rather abruptly. Only those with an adequate vessel and the proper experience should venture outside the bay.

Those going on their own should look for underwater structures, such as drop-offs or pinnacles. It helps to have a sonar unit or fish finder to locate the concentrations of fish that often congregate around these structures. Once they locate a spot, most fishermen use chunks of herring as bait or any one of a variety of jigs to attract these enormous flatfish. Because of the strong currents and the fish's size, it's common to use some pretty stout gear, usually a "tuna stick" with 80-pound braided Dacron line, and a sinker that often weighs a pound or two.

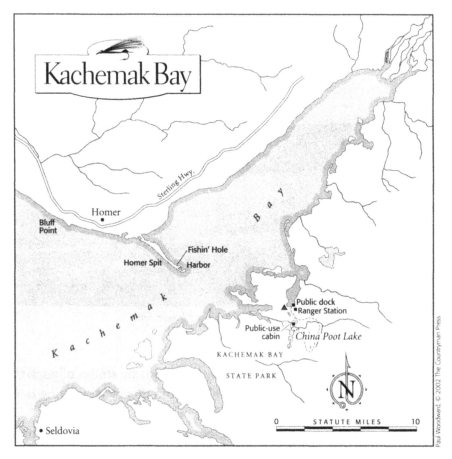

For those without a boat or the equipment, there are plenty of full- and half-day charters available. In fact, more than one hundred charter boats ply their trade out of this harbor, heading up to 40 miles outside Kachemak Bay in search of halibut. Most of these skippers know the halibut grounds well and will be able to find plenty of fish. But be prepared. You will often be fishing in water that is over 200 feet deep, with weights up to 4 or 5 pounds. This negates the fight of the average 30- or 40-pound halibut. But if you hook into a "barn door," one of those leviathans exceeding 200, even 300 pounds, watch out—you'll have your work cut out for you. When selecting a charter boat use the same criteria you would for any guide. Check references and, if possible, speak with your skipper and make sure you are comfortable before heading out. You also might want to purchase a ticket for the

The Fishin' Hole on the Homer Spit

Homer Jackpot Halibut Derby. Every year there are stories of anglers who didn't buy a ticket pulling in 300-pound monsters, missing out on their share of the $150,000 worth of prizes.

An option for those with small boats is to launch out of Anchor Point, 15 miles north of Homer, or off Deep Creek, near the village of Ninilchik. Halibut will come into this relatively shallow water to feed in April and May. Some fishermen drift, but most anchor and soak pieces of herring. Because of the exceptionally strong tides in Cook Inlet, many anglers fish only during the slack tide. Fortunately, king salmon are usually beginning to turn up in significant numbers about this time, and many anglers will bring two sets of gear and troll for kings between tides. They use the same trolling techniques described in chapter 15, often on an incoming tide, which draws the salmon closer to shore. Because the salmon are in close and in fairly shallow water, a sinker of 1 or 2 ounces is usually adequate.

There are commercially run tractor launches at both Anchor Point and Ninilchik. It is a good idea, for the sake of safety, to use them. It can be treacherous trying to launch or retrieve a boat in the surf, let alone the damage salt water can do to a vehicle. Old hands know that if the sea is rough, it is best to take your boat out during a falling tide. That way, if there is trouble, you will be left high and dry, rather than being pounded by the surf.

There are a large number of charter boats that operate both out of Ninilchik and Anchor Point, often providing combination salmon/halibut trips. Check with the guide first, but if your party has chartered the entire boat most skippers are amenable to fishing light gear for halibut. It can be an incredible amount of fun fishing for halibut with a much more nimble jigging rod and 30-pound-test line. Some fly-fishers have even taken to fishing for halibut with a 12-weight rod, sinking line, and a herring imitation. Of course, fishing light gear has its risks, such as not boating as many fish or losing a big one. Although you may need to assure your captain that you know these risks before he or she is willing to take you out with light tackle, many actually welcome the opportunity of doing something different.

As with any marine fishery, if you haven't operated a boat in the ocean before, it is wise to head out the first few times with an experienced skipper. This is especially true in a place like Cook Inlet, with so much open water and its vastly fluctuating tides.

Heading back to Kachemak Bay, there are fishing opportunities in abundance. Rockfish can be found along any of the steep outcroppings and boulder-strewn shorelines on the southwest side of the bay, as well as around the islands that dot the coastline. Dolly Varden migrate in close to shore in May and June and can be taken on light tackle, with spinners and streamer flies, off the Homer Spit.

Because of the mild coastal temperature (by Alaskan standards), king salmon fishing is popular throughout the year. In the winter, anglers troll for "feeder" kings, those migrating salmon that are not yet ready to spawn. They fish deep, often with downriggers, always keeping a lookout for congregations of seagulls feeding on the same baitfish that attract salmon. Trolling typically heats up in late April, as kings begin passing through, on their way to spawn in area streams. Fishing usually continues strong from June through July, with the best trolling taking place along the bluffs north of town or at the mouths of the small bays on the southern shore.

In order to increase angling opportunities, the Department of Fish and Game has planted various species of salmon around Kachemak Bay. King salmon are regularly stocked in Halibut Cove Lagoon, 12 miles southeast of the Homer Spit, and also near the village of Seldovia, 20 miles southwest of Homer. These fish, weighing up to 40 pounds, return in mid-May and run through early July, peaking in mid-June. Fishermen will have good luck early in the season casting artificial lures, and later with globs of salmon eggs or herring pieces suspended below the surface with a bobber. Sometime after the peak of the return, Fish and Game will open these stocks to snagging, which is usually done with large weighted treble hooks. This is definitely not most people's idea of fishing. These salmon, however, have nowhere to go—they are simply going to die—and this is a very efficient way to harvest them. Those looking strictly for sport may want to check with the Department of Fish and Game to see when snagging is taking place and fish elsewhere during this time.

King fishing in Seldovia takes place, for the most part, in town, at the harbor, or at the nearby slough. This quaint Alaskan village is definitely worth a visit. Small planes make the flight every day and there is a regular water taxi service that runs throughout the summer. Boaters choosing to head to Halibut Cove Lagoon should be aware that access is through a narrow channel and can only be made at high tide. Many unwary sailors have had to spend nearly half a day, or night, waiting for the tide to change before they are able to leave. State Parks maintains a campground here, as well as several public-use cabins that can be reserved through their office in Homer. There are also miles of hiking trails, including the trail to China Poot Lake. This lake, also known as Leisure Lake, has its own public-use cabin and contains rainbow trout, providing a nice respite from the rigors of salt-water fishing.

Kings, along with silver salmon, have also been planted at the Homer Spit, in a constructed lagoon commonly referred to as the Fishin' Hole. The kings run from May through early July, and the silvers from late July to mid-September. Inside the Fishin' Hole, it is strictly combat fishing, with snagging allowed periodically. Many anglers, in order to beat the crowd, will cast brightly colored spinners and spoons near the inlet to the Fishin' Hole or along the eastern side of the Spit. Trolling along this shore or soaking salmon egg clusters or cut herring is also popular.

Red salmon have been introduced into China Poot Bay, located 4 miles from Homer, on the southern side of Kachemak Bay. They arrive in large concentrations in the southeastern arm of the bay, from early July until mid-August, and can be taken in China Poot Creek with brightly colored streamer flies.

Pink salmon are plentiful and spawn in most streams on the southern side of Kachemak Bay. They can be caught in, or just outside, these streams, as well as along the Homer Spit. Pinks normally begin showing up in July and run well into August. The largest concentration of these salmon can be found in Tutka Lagoon, near the Tutka Hatchery, 15 miles southwest of town. This is an excellent opportunity to catch large numbers of fish on light tackle. There is a public-use cabin located about a mile outside of the lagoon, but the lagoon has a narrow entrance and can only be entered at high tide, so use caution.

Finding a Place to Stay

The accommodations available in Homer range from elegant to utterly simple. Even on the Homer Spit you can rent a luxury suite or pitch your tent along miles of gravel beach. There are a large number of excellent restaurants in town, many featuring local seafood and an incomparable view. There are also a variety of services available, including charters, water taxis, drop-offs at area beaches, kayak rentals, and all kinds of guided trips.

Most of the southern side of the bay, that entire panorama of magnificent mountains and shoreline across from Homer, is part of Kachemak Bay State Park—nearly 400,000 acres of forest, glaciers, and sea. Camping is allowed in most areas. There are also developed campsites scattered throughout the park, some with outhouses, fire-pits, picnic tables, and tent platforms. There are a number of public-use cabins as well—in Halibut Cove Lagoon, Tutka Bay, and on the shores of China Poot Lake. Most have mooring buoys nearby, and there is even an 80-foot-long public dock in Halibut Cove Lagoon. These cabins are popular; arrangements with Alaska State Parks must be made early to hold a reservation.

Along with excellent fishing, visitors often have the opportunity to see seals, porpoise, sea otters, and even whales. Eagles, moose, black bears, and wolves also frequent the area. It is a true wilderness, and we should all enter it prepared. Prepared not only for our own safety, prepared not only to have fun, but prepared to treat it with the respect it deserves, to leave this natural wonder as close as we can to the way we found it. It's the duty of all of us who hunt and fish, and who love the outdoors.

CHAPTER 17

Cooking Your Catch

I would implore anyone who cares about our resources, especially our freshwater fisheries, to practice catch-and-release when it comes to native rainbow trout and Dolly Varden. The areas they live, in comparison to the ocean, are small and very heavily fished. Salmon and groundfish stocks, however, are so closely monitored and abundant in Alaska, that in most areas of the state there are very healthy populations and plenty to go around. And one of life's great joys, after all, is a freshly caught king salmon just off the grill. So, with that in mind, here is a sampling of some tried-and-true recipes.

Smoked Salmon Canapés

3-oz. package cream cheese, softened
2 tablespoons sour cream
2 tablespoons mayonnaise
1 clove garlic, put through garlic press
Salt and pepper to taste
½ cup smoked salmon
crackers

A good day of fishing

Mix all ingredients except salmon. Flake the salmon and mix it in. Refrigerate the mixture for several hours, preferably overnight. Serve in a nice bowl with crackers on the side. It's a real crowd pleaser.

Baked Salmon or Halibut

½ cup mayonnaise
½ cup canned shredded Parmesan cheese (in most other recipes I prefer fresh Parmesan, but not in this case.)
1 tablespoon Dijon mustard
Large halibut or salmon fillet

Preheat the oven to 350 degrees.
Mix the mayonnaise, cheese, and mustard well. Spread the mixture ¼- to ½-inch thick over the fillet.
Place the fillet into the oven and bake for about 30 minutes. The fish is usually done about the time the topping begins to slightly brown, but check periodically with a fork to see if fish is flaky. Be careful not to overcook.

Grilled Salmon

Salmon
Lowery's Seasoned Salt
Butter, melted
Soy sauce

It sounds simple, but this is the best recipe I've ever found for grilling salmon over charcoal.
First, fillet your salmon, leaving the skin on. About an hour before you cook it, sprinkle the fish liberally with Lowery's Seasoned Salt. Then, about 20 minutes before grilling, brush a mixture of equal parts melted butter and soy sauce over the fillet. Place it onto the rack skin-side-down. Do NOT flip the fillet. Cover the grill, so the fish will cook from above as well as below. You may want to partially close the vents on your grill, depending on which type you have. Cook for about ½

hour, brushing the butter–soy sauce mixture over the fish once or twice while it's grilling. Check periodically with a fork for flakiness. It makes my mouth water just thinking about it.

Good luck and good fishing.

Index

A

Alaska Department of Fish and
   Game, 29
Alaska Fly Fishers, 29
Alaska Outdoor Journal, 29
Alaska State Parks, Kenai Area
   Office, 28–29
Anchor River
   accessing, 150–151
   overview of, 147–148
   tips for fishing, 148–150

B

Backbouncing, 126–127
Backtrolling, 125–126
Baked Salmon or Halibut recipe,
   183
Bears
   avoiding confrontations with, 24,
   26
   carrying firearms, 26
   responding to encounters with,
   26
Bench Lake, 71, 73
Binoculars, 21
Breeze Lake, 57
Burbot, 65

C

Cabin Lake, 89
Cabins, reserving, 27–29
Cameras, 21
Camp Island Lake, 60
Campers Lake, 61
Canoe Lake, 58

Carter Lake, 80
Centennial Lake, 90
Char
   Camp Island Lake, 60
   Gene Lake, 61
   Stormy Lake, 90
Chinook salmon. See King (chi-
   nook) salmon
Chugach National Forest, 28
Clam Lake, 59
Clothing, 21–23
Coho salmon. See Silver (coho)
   salmon
Combat fishing, 131–132
Cook Inlet. See Kachemak Bay and
   Cook Inlet
Crescent Lake
   accessing, 79–80
   cycling to, 75–77, 79
   map of, 78
   tips for fishing, 80
Crooked Creek, 145, 147
Crooked Creek Campground,
   146

D

Dabbler Lake, 57
Daniels Lake, 89
Day packs, 21
Dead drifting, 113–114, 117, 119
Deep Creek
   accessing, 150–151
   overview of, 147–148
   tips for fishing, 148–150

Devil's Pass Lake, 66
Dolly Varden trout
    Anchor River, 147–151
    Daniels Lake, 89
    Deep Creek, 147–151
    Devil's Pass Lake, 66
    Engineer Lake, 88
    Grouse Lake, 87
    Hidden Lake, 88
    Jean Lake, 87
    Jerome Lake, 86
    Kachemak Bay and Cook Inlet, 173–180
    Kenai River, 105, 112–114, 117, 119, 121–122
    Lower Russian Lake, 68
    Lower Trail Lake, 87
    making the catch of a lifetime, 34–36
    Ninilchik River, 147–151
    Ohmer Lakes, 88
    Ptarmigan Creek, 142–143
    Quartz Creek, 142–143
    Resurrection Bay (Seward), 163–171
    Russian River, 137–142
    Summit Lakes, 85–86
    Swan Lake, 59, 66
    Tern Lake, 87
    Upper Trail Lake, 87
Drake Lake, 57
Dry bags, 21

E
Egumen Lake, 88–89
Engineer Lake, 88
Esposito, Nick, 42–45

F
Firearms, carrying, 26

Fly-fishing
    being willing to try other methods, 11
    cooking your catch, 181, 183–184
    discovering the wonders of, 31–34
    making the catch of a lifetime, 34–36
Forceps, 21
Forest Lake, 57

G
Gavia Lake, 58
Gene Lake, 60–63
Gloves, 22
Grayling
    Bench Lake, 73
    Crescent Lake, 80
    Grayling Lake, 81
    Lower Fuller Lake, 80–81
    Lower Paradise Lake, 82–83
    Upper Paradise Lake, 82–83
Grayling Lake, 81
Grilled Salmon recipe, 183–184
Grouse Lake, 87
Guides, selecting, 23–24

H
Halibut
    Kachemak Bay and Cook Inlet, 173–180
    Resurrection Bay (Seward), 163–171
Hats, 22
Hidden Lake, 88
Hidden Lake Campground, 88
Homer. See Kachemak Bay and Cook Inlet
Hook hones, 21

Humpback salmon. *See* Pink
  (humpback) salmon

I
Ilerun Lake, 64
Insect repellent, 21

J
Jean Lake, 87
Jerome Lake, 86
Johnson Lake, 71, 90
Johnson Pass Trail
  Bench Lake, 71, 73
  Johnson Lake, 71
  map of, 72
Juneau Lake, 65

K
Kachemak Bay and Cook Inlet
  appreciating the beauty of
    Homer, 173–174
  Dolly Varden, 177
  finding a place to stay, 179–180
  halibut, 174–177
  Homer Jackpot Halibut Derby,
    175–176
  king (chinook) salmon, 176–179
  map of, 175
  pink (humpback) salmon, 179
  red (sockeye) salmon, 179
  silver (coho) salmon, 178–179
  tips for fishing, 174–179
Kachemak Bay State Park, 179–180
Kasilof River
  map of, 146
  overview of, 145–146
  tips for fishing, 146–147
Kelly Lake, 88
Kelso, Richard, 75–77, 93–97
Kenai Fjords National Park, 29
Kenai National Wildlife Refuge, 29

Kenai River
  accessing, 122–123
  as Alaska's most famous fishery,
    105, 107
  catching king (chinook) salmon
    backbouncing, 126–127
    backtrolling, 125–126
    drifting, 127
    fly-fishing tips, 127–128
    runs, 105, 124, 125
    salmon characteristics,
      124–125
  catching pink (humpback)
    salmon
    salmon characteristics,
      134–135
    tips on, 105, 135
  catching rainbow trout and
    Dolly Varden
    dead drifting, 113–114, 117,
      119
    fishing after the mid-June
      reopening, 121–122
    fishing before the May 1 clo-
      sure, 121
    late season fishing, 122
    using a slinky fly, 113, 114
    using egg patterns, 121–122
    using flesh flies, 122
    using plugs, 113
  catching red (sockeye) salmon
    combat fishing, 131–132
    fly-fishing tips, 130–131
    runs, 105, 124, 129
    salmon characteristics,
      129–130
    using the Kenai flip, 130,
      131
  catching silver (coho) salmon
    backtrolling, 133

fly-fishing tips, 133–134
runs, 105, 124, 133
salmon characteristics,
    132–133
using spinners and spoons,
    133
hiring a guide for, 123
keeping what you catch, 123
Lower Kenai River, 111–112
maps of, 106, 108, 110, 112
Middle Kenai River, 109–111
Upper Kenai River, 107–109
variety of fishing experiences on,
    107
King (chinook) salmon
Anchor River, 147–151
Deep Creek, 147–151
Kachemak Bay and Cook Inlet,
    173–180
Kasilof River, 145–147
Kenai River, 105, 124–128
Ninilchik River, 147–151
Resurrection Bay (Seward),
    163–171
King Lake, 64
Kokanee salmon, 88
Konchanee Lake, 58

L
Lake fishing. *See also* specific lakes
dry flies for, 52–53
enjoying the still-water wonder-
    land, 41–45
fishing more than one fly,
    54
fly rods and line for, 52
looking for where fish rest, feed,
    and migrate, 47–49
marking your map and keeping a
    log, 49

relative constancy of lakes, 49
spinning gear for, 52
streamers for, 54
using a float tube or canoe,
    51
varying your retrieve, 54
Lake trout
Hidden Lake, 88
Juneau Lake, 65
Lower Trail Lake, 87
Swan Lake, 66
Trout Lake, 64
Upper Trail Lake, 87
Lewis, Tony, 95
Loon Lake, 59
Lost Lake, 62
Lower Fuller Lake, 80–81
Lower Kenai River
map of, 112
overview of, 111–112
Lower Paradise Lake, 82–83
Lower Russian Lake, 67–68
Lower Russian River, 138–139
Lower Trail Lake, 87
Lynx Lake, 64

M
McCrossan, Bill, 43–45
McDonnell, Jerry, 93, 97
Middle Kenai River
map of, 110
overview of, 109, 111
Moose River, 59
Moosehorn Lake, 59
Muse, Curt, 114

N
Nest Lake, 57
Ninilchik River
accessing, 150–151

overview of, 147–148
tips for fishing, 148–150
Nuthatch Lake, 63, 64

O
Ohmer Lakes, 88

P
Paddle Lake, 60
Paradise Lakes, 82–83
Pepper Lake, 61, 63
Peterson Lake, 88
Pink (humpback) salmon
  Kachemak Bay and Cook Inlet,
    173–180
  Kenai River, 105, 124, 134–135
  Resurrection Bay (Seward),
    163–171
  Resurrection Creek, 159–160
Planning your trip
  avoiding areas with recent bear
    activity, 24
  beginning early, 19
  being prepared for changes in
    weather, 21–22
  dealing with congestion, 20
  doing your research, 27–29
  having backup plans, 19–20
  important items to bring, 21–23
  reserving a cabin, 27–29
  responding to changing fishing
    conditions, 19–20
  selecting a guide, 23–24
  wearing proper clothing, 21–23
Pliers, 21
Portage Lake, 58
Ptarmigan Creek, 142–143

Q
Quartz Creek, 142–143
Quinn, Jim, 41–45

R
Rainbow trout
  Cabin Lake, 89
  Camp Island Lake, 60
  Carter Lake, 80
  Centennial Lake, 90
  Clam Lake, 59
  Daniels Lake, 89
  Egumen Lake, 89
  Engineer Lake, 88
  Gene Lake, 61
  Hidden Lake, 88
  Jean Lake, 87
  Jerome Lake, 86
  Johnson Lake, 71, 90
  Juneau Lake, 65
  Kelly Lake, 88
  Kenai River, 105, 112–114, 117,
    119, 121–122
  Loon Lake, 59
  Lower Paradise Lake, 82
  Lower Russian Lake, 68
  Lower Trail Lake, 87
  Moosehorn Lake, 59
  Ohmer Lakes, 88
  Peterson Lake, 88
  Ptarmigan Creek, 142–143
  Quartz Creek, 142–143
  Russian River, 137–142
  Scout Lake, 90
  Stormy Lake, 90
  Swan Lake, 66
  Swanson River, 158–159
  Trout Lake, 64
  Upper Russian Lake, 70
  Upper Trail Lake, 87
  Vagt Lake, 87
  Watson Lake, 89
Raingear, 21–22
Rating system, 13

Recipes, 181, 183–184
Red Lake, 61–62
Red (sockeye) salmon
Kachemak Bay and Cook Inlet, 173–180
Kasilof River, 145–147
Kenai River, 105, 124, 129–132
Russian River, 137–142
Swanson River, 158–159
Resurrection Bay (Seward)
appreciating the beauty of, 163, 165
Dolly Varden, 168–169
finding a place to stay, 170–171
going after rockfish, 169–170
halibut, 169
king (chinook) salmon, 169
map of, 164
renting a skiff, 165–166
Seward Silver Salmon Derby, 165
silver (coho) salmon, 166, 168
tips for fishing, 166, 168–170
Resurrection Creek, 159–160
Resurrection Pass Trail
Devil's Pass Lake, 66
Juneau Lake, 65
map of, 65
Swan Lake, 66
Trout Lake, 64
River and stream fishing. See also specific rivers and streams
matching equipment/techniques to time of year, water type, and target species, 102
pushing the season, 93–97
surveying the situation, 99, 101–102
viewing the river in parts and as a whole, 102–103

Russian Lakes Trail
Lower Russian Lake, 67–68
map of, 67
Upper Russian Lake, 68–71
Russian River
Lower Russian River, 138–139
overview of, 137–138
Upper Russian River, 140–142
Russian River Campground, 67

S
Salmon. See individual species
Salt water fishing. See specific bodies of water
Scout Lake, 90
Seward. See Resurrection Bay (Seward)
Silver (coho) salmon
Anchor River, 147–151
Deep Creek, 147–151
Kachemak Bay and Cook Inlet, 173–180
Kasilof River, 145–147
Kenai River, 105, 124, 132–134
Ninilchik River, 147–151
Resurrection Bay (Seward), 163–171
Russian River, 137–142
Swanson River, 158–159
Silver salmon (landlocked)
Centennial Lake, 90
Engineer Lake, 88
Johnson Lake, 90
Scout Lake, 90
Skookum Lake, 57
Smoked Salmon Canapés recipe, 181, 183
Sockeye salmon. See Red (sockeye) salmon
Socks, 22–23

Spruce Lake, 58, 59
Squirrel Lake, 62
Steelhead
    Anchor River, 147–151
    Crooked Creek, 145, 147
    Deep Creek, 147–151
    experiencing the wonder and
      power of, 95–96
    Ninilchik River, 147–151
Stormy Lake, 89
Stream fishing. *See* River and
    stream fishing
Summit Lakes, 85–86
Sunglasses, 21
Swan Lake, 59, 66
Swan Lake/Swanson River Canoe
    System
    accessing the system, 55
    fishing the roadside lakes
        Breeze Lake, 57
        Dabbler Lake, 57
        Drake Lake, 57
        Forest Lake, 57
        Nest Lake, 57
        pressure on the lakes, 55, 57
        Skookum Lake, 57
    Swan Lake Route
        Camp Island Lake, 60
        Canoe Lake, 58
        Central Passage, 59–60
        Clam Lake, 59
        Gavia Lake, 58
        Konchanee Lake, 58
        lakes with no fish, 59, 60
        Loon Lake, 59
        map of, 58
        Moosehorn Lake, 59
        North Passage, 58–59
        Portage Lake, 58
        Spruce Lake, 58, 59

    Swan Lake, 59
    Trout Lake, 58
    West Passage, 60
    Swanson River Route
        Campers Lake, 61
        Gene Lake, 60–63
        Ilerun Lake, 64
        King Lake, 64
        lakes with no fish, 64
        Lost Lake, 62
        Lynx Lake, 64
        map of, 62
        Nuthatch Lake, 63, 64
        Paddle Lake, 60
        Pepper Lake, 61, 63
        Red Lake, 61–62
        Squirrel Lake, 62
        Swanson Lake, 61
        Wilderness Lake, 63, 64
        Woods Lake, 61–62
Swanson Lake, 61
Swanson River
    as a quiet alternative, 153,
      155–157, 159
    tips for fishing, 158–159

T
Tern Lake, 87
Trip planning. *See* Planning your
    trip
Trout. *See* individual species
Trout Lake, 58, 64

U
Upper Kenai River
    map of, 108
    overview of, 107, 109
Upper Paradise Lake, 82–83
Upper Russian Lake
    overview of, 68–70

tips for fishing, 70–71

Upper Russian River, 140–142

Upper Trail Lake, 87

U.S. Fish and Wildlife Service,
Kenai National Wildlife Refuge,
29

U.S. Forest Service, Chugach
National Forest, 28

V

Vagt Lake, 87

W

Waders, 21

Watson Lake, 89

Weather, being prepared for
changes in, 21–22

Wilderness Lake, 63, 64

Wildlife
avoiding confrontations with, 24,
26

carrying firearms, 26

as part of what makes Alaska
great, 24

respecting, 26

responding to encounters with,
26

Woods Lake, 61–62

CPSIA information can be obtained
at www.ICGtesting.com
Printed in the USA
LVHW021229010421
683211LV00003B/310